ALSO BY ROBIN MILLER

The Newlywed Cookbook
Robin Takes 5 for Busy Families
Robin Takes 5
Robin to the Rescue
Robin Rescues Dinner
Quick Fix Meals
Picnics
Verdure
The Daily Soup
Jane Fonda, Cooking for Healthy Living

30-MINUTE

Meal Prep

100 HEALTHY AND DELICIOUS RECIPES TO EAT ALL WEEK

ROBIN MILLER

This publication is designed to provide accurate and authoritative information in regard
to the subject matter covered. It is sold with the understanding that the publisher is not
engaged in rendering legal, accounting, or other professional service. If legal advice
or other expert assistance is required, the services of a competent professional person
should be sought.—From a Declaration of Principles Jointly Adopted by a Committee
of the American Bar Association and a Committee of Publishers and Associations

Published by Sourcebooks
P.O. Box 4410, Naperville, Illinois 60567-4410
(630) 961-3900
sourcebooks.com

Cataloging-in-Publication Data is on file with the Library of Congress.

Printed and bound in the United States of America.
POD

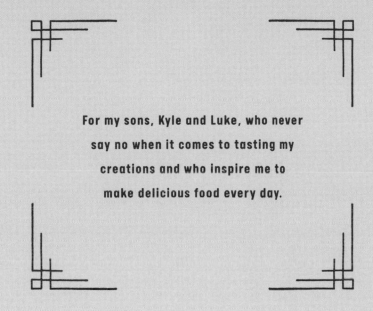

For my sons, Kyle and Luke, who never
say no when it comes to tasting my
creations and who inspire me to
make delicious food every day.

Table of Contents

PASTA AND RICE — 187

Introduction

Can this be real? A cookbook that promises 30-minute meal prep for every single dish? Yes. You now have one hundred new reasons to make dinner—meals you can serve in 30 minutes max. In many cases, dinner will be on the table much faster than that.

I wrote this cookbook for one reason: to solve your dinner dilemma. But I didn't stop there. This essential resource tackles nightly meals and weekly meal planning as well as providing strategies for setting up your pantry.

My life is a lot like yours—a daily juggle of work, family, errands, and chores. And hobbies if I'm lucky. All that and I didn't mention dinner, which clearly needs to be addressed. Turn the page and you'll quickly realize the "dinner problem" is solved.

I didn't just write one hundred recipes I think you'll love. I know you'll adore the food. But I understand you need more, so I've shared my strategies for effortlessly transforming everyday ingredients into mind-blowing meals. And get this: leftovers from half of those meals transition into completely different, equally outstanding dinners. I can tell you this with confidence: this is an *indispensable resource* for all busy home cooks (me included) because it makes mealtime simpler, your life easier, and the whole cooking experience better—which makes everyone happier.

Smack in the front of this cookbook, you'll find Meal Prep 101: twenty-five tactics that will revolutionize your experience in the kitchen. From how to prep ingredients to what to stash in your pantry, you'll find life-altering suggestions that will change your approach to mealtime.

Then, it's on to the recipes. I've compiled a collection of meals that will inspire you. I want you to gaze at that package of chicken with enthusiasm, not apathy; a pound of beef with gusto, not gloom. And that box of pasta deserves excitement, not indifference. As you read through these recipes, you'll soon agree—you can create mouthwatering, wholesome, family-friendly meals with a handful of ingredients in under 30 minutes. Oh, and after one meal is complete, you're teed up for a future meal. Read on.

There's a strategy behind how the recipes in this book are written. In each chapter, you'll find "Round One" recipes and "Round Two" recipes. Working with leftovers is an integral part of my planning-ahead strategy, and this scheme not only takes the stress out of meal planning, but it also streamlines the cooking process for 50 percent of

the recipes in this book. What happens if you're craving a Round Two dish and you didn't make Round One? Don't fret; every Round Two recipe can be made without repurposing leftovers.

I truly hope you dive into this cookbook with passion and excitement, knowing that you've got the recipes, tips, and strategies to create fabulous meals with ease. With a few tricks up your sleeve (and some leftovers in the fridge), mealtime can be wholly rewarding.

One more thing: it's great when everyone raves about delicious food, but remember this— your amazing meal may have made it to the table quickly and easily, but more importantly, it was shared with the people you love. Bon appétit.

Meal Prep 101

Below you will find twenty-five quick-and-easy strategies for creating an efficient, well-organized kitchen—a culinary workspace designed to simplify meal planning and preparation. These tips and tactics are easy to incorporate into your lifestyle, and they will have a profound impact on dinnertime. Choose a few concepts or choose them all, but one thing is certain: when you take the time to plan ahead, meal preparation takes no time at all.

Twenty-Five Strategies for Creating a Well-Appointed, Perfectly Functional Kitchen and Pantry

1. CHOP VEGETABLES YOU REGULARLY USE AND REFRIGERATE THEM IN SEALABLE CONTAINERS OR PLASTIC BAGS UNTIL READY TO USE. Many recipes for sauces, soups, stews, and chilies start with aromatics like onions, carrots, celery, bell peppers, and garlic, so chop your produce in advance (up to 4 days) and it will be ready when you are. This strategy can easily slash 15 to 20 minutes from your daily prep time.

2. MEASURE INTERNATIONALLY INSPIRED SPICE BLENDS AND STORE THEM IN CONTAINERS OR JARS FOR UP TO 6 MONTHS. For an Italian medley, combine oregano, basil, thyme, rosemary, and marjoram. For a Mexican/Southwest mix, combine chili powder (regular or hot), cumin, cilantro, and oregano. For Asian inspiration, combine garlic, sesame seeds, ginger, and a pinch of cinnamon. For an all-purpose

Mediterranean seasoning, combine parsley, oregano, basil, fennel, dill, cumin, and paprika.

3. **MEASURE AND PREP INGREDIENTS BEFORE YOU START COOKING.** The recipes in this cookbook are ready in a flash, so it helps to have all your ingredients measured, chopped, and prepped before you start cooking. It's never ideal when the oil in your skillet starts smoking before you've finished chopping. Yes, I've done it too.

4. **MEASURE INGREDIENTS FROM DRY TO WET.** We've all been there, rinsing dried herbs from an oil-slicked measuring spoon. As with most recipes, the ingredients in this cookbook are listed in the order in which they are used. That means you might find the oregano after the olive oil, or the panko breadcrumbs after the yogurt. Measure the dry ingredients first and you'll save the rinsing step between wet and dry. *Dry before wet and rinsing is offset.*

5. **WHEN MAKING SAUCES AND MARINADES, DOUBLE OR TRIPLE THE RECIPE AND RESERVE LEFTOVERS FOR FUTURE MEALS.** Store sauces and marinades in sealable containers or freezer bags and they will last up to 5 days in the refrigerator or up to 3 months in the freezer. Your future self will thank you for having comforting, homemade sauces and marinades on hand, especially on busy weeknights. Great examples include pasta sauce, meat sauce, gravies, Asian glazes, and marinades for chicken, steak, pork, and seafood.

6. **WHEN MAKING CASSEROLES, PREPARE TWO INSTEAD OF ONE.** For example, if you have all the ingredients out and ready for lasagna, assemble two complete casseroles and freeze the second one (before baking) for up to 3 months. Thaw frozen casseroles overnight in the refrigerator and then bake as directed. This works will all types of casseroles, from the classic tuna noodle to traditional enchiladas.

7. **WHEN ROASTING CHICKEN BREASTS, TENDERS, OR THIGHS, DOUBLE THE AMOUNT AND RESERVE THE LEFTOVERS FOR ANOTHER NIGHT.** Cooked chicken is a quick cook's best friend and will last up to 4 days in the refrigerator and 3 months in the freezer. What should you do with the leftover chicken? The possibilities are endless. Just know that by starting with cooked chicken, you'll shed *at least* 10 to 15 minutes from your meal prep time. What do I mean by prep time and cook time? Prep time is the time it takes for you to get your ingredients ready, such as chopping onions and measuring herbs. Cook time is the amount of time food is heated, either on the cooktop or in the oven. Those two combined will be 30 minutes or less. Great ideas include chicken fried rice, chicken burritos, pizza with chicken and vegetables, chicken salad, chicken Caesar wraps, and practically every casserole that calls for cooked poultry.

8. **FREEZE INDIVIDUAL PORTIONS OF LEFTOVERS, NOT JUST ENTIRE CASSEROLES.** How many times have you opened your freezer and wished you had something to serve two people when all you have is a casserole big enough to serve six? When you freeze in smaller portions, thawing is quicker (and safer), and you can serve one or two people with ease.

9. **LABEL AND DATE EVERYTHING.** No more mystery food in the icebox! When packing up food for the freezer, add the description and date. Although you think you might remember the contents, once food is frozen, it's hard to decipher what it is. Try to thaw and enjoy all frozen food within 3 months (this is a food *quality* tip, not a food *safety* issue).

10. **GET CREATIVE WITH SALAD DRESSINGS AND VINAIGRETTES.** Bottled dressings and vinaigrettes are typically crammed with tasty ingredients, including robust vinegars, mustards, oils, herbs, and spices. Take advantage of this one-stop flavor shop and consider using them as the base of your sauces and marinades.

11. **MAKE YOUR CONDIMENTS DO DOUBLE DUTY.** Just like dressings and vinaigrettes, chutneys, relishes, pesto, miso paste, and other condiments can be precious time-savers on a busy weeknight. You can either use these pantry staples as the base of your sauces and marinades or use them as quick-and-easy toppings/garnishes just before serving.

12. **LOAD UP ON TOMATOES OF ALL KINDS.** Canned tomatoes might be one of the most important ingredients in your pantry armory. They come in a variety of forms and can be used in sauces, soups, stews, salads, and more. Regular, fire-roasted, seasoned, diced, pureed, crushed, and sauced, tomatoes add great flavor, color, nutrition, and heft to countless meals.

13. **FILL A SHELF WITH CANNED BEANS.** In case you haven't noticed, the canned bean section of the grocery store has exploded over the last few years. Not only can you find traditional canned beans of all colors (black, white, pink, and red kidney beans), you can find tender legumes swimming in seasoned sauces (great for stews, soups, chilies, and even nachos). And when it comes to stretching meals, canned beans are your huckleberry—they're filling, affordable, and rich in protein and fiber.

14. **BUY SHREDDED CHEESE AND/OR BUY A BLOCK OF CHEESE AND SHRED IT YOURSELF.** Shredded cheese is an essential time-saver, but the convenience item is often pricier than cheese sold whole. Keep some shredded cheese on hand for ultra-busy weeknights, and when possible, shred or grate whole blocks of cheese just before serving. Note that pre-shredded cheese contains additives (like potato starch) used to keep the shreds from clumping and sticking together in the package. Those additives also prevent the cheese from melting as smoothly as cheese you shred yourself. Pre-shredded cheese still melts, and it's great for toppings, but for things like cream sauce, the final result might not be as satiny as sauce made with freshly shredded cheese.

15. **BROTHS AND BOUILLON ADD GREAT FLAVOR IN A SNAP.** Whether you're making a soup, stew, sauce, or gravy, ready-to-use broths, bouillon cubes, and jarred bouillon add great flavor in minutes. Once open, liquid broths have a limited shelf life (in the refrigerator), so keep the cubes on hand as a backup.

16. **NEVER RUN OUT OF QUICK-COOKING GRAINS.** Fast-cooking grains like rice, quinoa, and couscous not only make excellent side dishes, but they can also become the base of nutritious, complete meals.

17. **WASH HERBS AS SOON AS YOU GET HOME FROM THE GROCERY STORE.** This might not be your favorite tip (adding more work to your to-do list as you unpack the groceries) but trust me. Fresh herbs are often used at the end of cooking—just before serving—a time when you're hustling to get to the table. Being able to grab prewashed herbs and give them a quick chop (or simply pull some leaves) is an excellent time-saver. You'll thank me later for this one.

18. **DON'T LET YOUR BERRIES GET PAST THEIR PRIME.** Fresh berries are a superb addition to all types of dishes, from your morning cereal to your dinner salads and desserts. But they don't last very long! Before they turn the corner and become inedible, give fresh berries a rinse under cold water and spread them out on a baking sheet to freeze (for bananas, simply peel them and add them to the baking sheet). Once frozen, store the fruit in freezer bags and use it in smoothies, muffins, quick breads, and other baked treats.

19. **COOK BACON IN ADVANCE AND FREEZE IT.** There are many reasons this is an awesome tip. First, you can roast an entire package of bacon in just minutes and dodge a stove top full of grease. Second, you'll always have cooked bacon nearby. To roast bacon, arrange the strips on a parchment-lined baking sheet in a single layer. Roast at 400°F for 12 to 15 minutes, until chewy-crisp. Blot the bacon with paper towels, and freeze in a freezer bag for up to 3 months. When you're ready for bacon (either for breakfast or as a garnish), pull as many slices as you need and reheat, without thawing, in a 300°F oven for 5 to 10 minutes (or in the microwave for 30 to 60 seconds).

20. **SALVAGE BREAD BY TURNING IT INTO CROUTONS.** Don't toss old bread just because it's hard and dry. Bread that's no longer soft is perfect for cubing and making croutons. To make the salad topper, cube the bread and toss it with melted butter or olive oil (enough to coat all sides). Then season with your favorite dried herbs, spread out on a baking sheet, and bake in a 375°F oven for 5 to 10 minutes, until golden and crisp.

21. **DEFROST OVERNIGHT IN THE FRIDGE, NOT ON THE COUNTER OR IN THE MICROWAVE.** This is a food-safety tip, but it's a good one. In absolute dire situations (when you need to thaw food fast), use a cold-water bath for 30 minutes. This speeds the thawing process for most frozen items, from chicken breasts to ground beef, to frozen seafood.

22. **CONSIDER SHEET PAN COOKING SO YOU CAN COOK ENTIRE MEALS AT ONCE.** One-pan meals are a busy cook's pal in the kitchen, and sheet pan meals require no hands-on work once the pan is in the oven (versus stove-top meals that require attention). Plus, if you've incorporated some of the other tips from this list (pre-chopping vegetables, using dressings as marinades, and washing herbs before storing), dinner prep will be a breeze.

23. **DON'T STRESS ABOUT SIDES.** Sometimes getting dinner on the table is a feat, so don't add work by crafting a complicated side dish. There's nothing wrong with steaming a bag of frozen green beans or opening a can of corn. Many recipes in this book provide serving suggestions, but for those without side dish ideas, keep it simple.

24. **PARTY APPETIZERS MAKE GREAT SIDE DISHES.** Stay with me here; this is a useful tip.

Don't relegate your crudités platter to special events. Raw vegetables and dip make an excellent, no-cook side dish option for any busy weeknight. The same is true of cheese and crackers, peanut butter–stuffed celery, cured meats like salami and pepperoni, and fresh fruit like grapes and sliced apples. These options are nutritious, filling, and ready in minutes. Younger members of the family will also love these side dishes.

25. **BREAD COUNTS AS A SIDE DISH.** Now you have the freedom to check another dinner item off your list. Side dish: done. There are countless varieties of delicious, wholesome breads at the grocery store, from freshly baked breads with seeds and whole grains to the minimally processed loaves found in the bread aisle. Don't relegate bread to sandwiches and toast; choose breads that are high in fiber and low in preservatives and added sugars, and you'll have an excellent, lightning-fast, whole grain side dish. To jazz things up, serve the bread with a little dish of olive oil for dipping (and season the oil with some fresh or dried rosemary if you're feeling extra gourmet).

CHICKEN

GOOD TO KNOW

In this recipe, I call for minced dried garlic, which is dehydrated garlic flakes. I find dried garlic a quick cook's best friend on nights when you don't have the time to peel and mince fresh cloves. When a recipe calls for fresh garlic, substitute ½ teaspoon minced dried garlic for each clove. If you have garlic powder, use ⅛ teaspoon powder for every clove of fresh garlic.

Italian Lemon Chicken

This ingredient list may be short, but flavors abound in this one-pan meal. After a quick marinade, the zingy chicken can be cooked indoors or outside on the grill, and the result is moist chicken that's brimming with tangy lemon, Italian seasoning, and garlic—fresh, light, and an excellent addition to your regular routine.

Serves 4, with leftover chicken for a future meal

10 minutes

15 minutes

¼ cup fresh lemon juice

2 tablespoons olive oil, plus more for coating the pan

2 teaspoons Italian seasoning

1 ½ teaspoons minced dried garlic, or ½ teaspoon garlic powder, or 3 cloves garlic, minced

1 teaspoon grated fresh lemon zest

Salt and freshly ground black pepper

6 boneless, skinless chicken breast halves, or 12 to 15 chicken tenders, or 12 thighs

Chopped fresh parsley for serving

1. In a shallow dish or large zip-top bag, combine the lemon juice, olive oil, Italian seasoning, garlic, lemon zest, ½ teaspoon salt, and ¼ teaspoon black pepper. Add the chicken, seal the bag, and turn to coat, pressing the marinade into the meat. If you have the time, marinate for 30 minutes or up to 8 hours in the refrigerator.

2. Coat an outdoor grill, grill pan, or skillet with olive oil, and preheat to medium-high. Remove the chicken from the marinade, discard the marinade, and add the chicken to the hot pan. Cook for 5 to 7 minutes per side, until the chicken is cooked through (a meat thermometer should register 165°F for all cuts of chicken; chicken tenders will cook a few minutes faster).

3. Reserve half of the chicken for the Easy Chicken Pot Pie (page 12) or another future meal. Refrigerate for up to 3 days.

4. Top the remaining chicken with fresh parsley and serve.

SERVING SUGGESTION: For a complete and filling meal, serve the chicken with your favorite raw or steamed vegetable and a starchy side, such as rice, beans, pasta, potatoes, sweet potatoes, quinoa, couscous, or whole grain bread. For more inspiration, check out Meal Prep 101 tips 23, 24, and 25.

Round Two

Easy Chicken Pot Pie

This deconstructed chicken pot pie is the ultimate comfort-food meal. The chunks of chicken are already seasoned, so there's no need to raid your spice rack to prepare this winning dish. Each spoonful features aromatic vegetables, herby sauce, tender chicken, and flaky buttermilk biscuits.

Serves 4

10 minutes

20 minutes

1 (6-ounce) container refrigerated biscuits (5 biscuits)

2 tablespoons unsalted butter

1 tablespoon olive oil

1 cup chopped carrots

1 cup chopped celery

1 cup chopped onion, any color

2 tablespoons all-purpose flour

Salt and freshly ground black pepper

2 cups chicken broth

4 cups diced cooked chicken from the Italian Lemon Chicken (page 11), or any cooked chicken

½ cup frozen corn, kept frozen until ready to use

½ cup frozen peas, kept frozen until ready to use

Chopped fresh parsley for serving, optional

1. Cook the biscuits according to the package directions.
2. Meanwhile, heat the butter and olive oil together in a large stock pot or saucepan over medium-high heat. Add the carrots, celery, and onion, and cook for 3 to 5 minutes, until soft.
3. Add the flour, ½ teaspoon salt, and ¼ teaspoon black pepper, and stir to coat.
4. Add the broth, and bring to a simmer. Add the chicken, reduce the heat to low, and simmer for 10 minutes, until the sauce thickens.
5. Add the corn and peas, and cook for 1 minute to heat through. Season to taste with salt and black pepper.
6. Ladle the stew into bowls, and top with the biscuits.
7. Top with fresh parsley (if using), and serve.

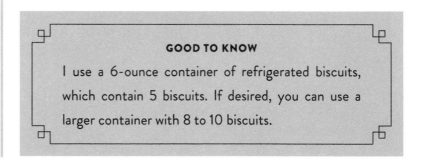

GOOD TO KNOW

I use a 6-ounce container of refrigerated biscuits, which contain 5 biscuits. If desired, you can use a larger container with 8 to 10 biscuits.

GOOD TO KNOW

This recipe recommends a dark Mexican beer for added richness. Feel free to use any beer you prefer.

Beer-Braised Chipotle Chicken

Smoky, tangy, and incredibly tender, this chicken is as amazing as it is easy. Store-bought chipotle chiles in adobo sauce make the base of the smoky sauce, and then everything is kicked up with tangy beer, garlic, dijon mustard, chili powder, and cumin. You need only one pan and a handful of ingredients, and you have the ultimate chicken dinner (with leftovers) at your fingertips.

Serves 4, with leftover chicken for a future meal

10 minutes

20 minutes

3 tablespoons minced chipotle chiles in adobo sauce

2 cloves garlic, minced, or ½ teaspoon garlic powder

1 teaspoon chili powder

1 teaspoon dijon mustard

½ teaspoon ground cumin

Salt and freshly ground black pepper

2 tablespoons olive oil or vegetable oil

2 pounds boneless, skinless chicken breast halves, tenders, or thighs

1 (12-ounce) beer, preferably a dark Mexican beer, such as Modelo, Trejo's Cerveza, or AleSmith, or beer of choice

Fresh cilantro leaves for serving

Chopped red onion for serving

1. In a large shallow dish, whisk together the chipotle chiles, garlic, chili powder, dijon mustard, cumin, 1 teaspoon salt, and ½ teaspoon black pepper. Add the chicken, and turn to coat. If you have the time, refrigerate for 1 hour or up to 24 hours.

2. Heat the olive oil (or vegetable oil) in a large, high-sided skillet over medium-high heat. Working in batches to prevent crowding the pan, add the chicken, and cook until golden brown on both sides, about 3 to 4 minutes per side. Return all the chicken to the pot, add the beer, and bring to a gentle boil. Reduce the heat to medium-low, partially cover, and simmer for 15 minutes, until you can easily shred the chicken with two forks.

3. Transfer the chicken to a plate, and shred with two forks.

4. Place the skillet back over medium heat, and simmer until the liquid reduces by about half. Return the chicken to the pan, and simmer for 1 to 2 minutes to heat through. Season to taste with salt and black pepper.

5. Reserve 2 cups of the chicken for the Buffalo Chicken Pizza (page 16) or another future meal. Refrigerate for up to 3 days.

6. Top the remaining chicken with fresh cilantro and red onions, and serve.

SERVING SUGGESTION: I suggest serving this buttery chicken in soft tortillas (corn or flour) or lettuce leaves or over your favorite grain, such as rice, couscous, quinoa, or farro.

Buffalo Chicken Pizza

My son Luke took one bite of this pizza and said, "Oh wow." That's pretty telling because he samples something new almost every day. Luke's reaction was spot on; each chewy, cheesy bite of this pizza is packed with flavor—from the toasty crust to the ranch-spiked ricotta, fiery shredded chicken, and buttery mozzarella cheese. It's a medley of flavor—first the heat, then the creamy dairy—and it's impossible to stop at one slice.

Serves 4

10 minutes

12 to 16 minutes

1 (13.8-ounce) container refrigerated pizza dough

1 cup ricotta cheese

3 tablespoons powdered ranch dip/dressing mix

2 cups shredded cooked chicken from the Beer-Braised Chipotle Chicken (page 15), or any cooked chicken

¼ cup hot sauce, such as Frank's, or hot sauce of choice

1 cup shredded mozzarella cheese

Chopped fresh chives for serving, optional

Bottled ranch dressing for serving, optional

1. Preheat the oven to 400°F. Line a large baking sheet with parchment paper or aluminum foil.

2. Unroll the pizza dough on the prepared pan, and shape as desired; I chose a 10-by-12-inch rectangle. Bake for 6 minutes.

3. Meanwhile, in a small bowl, combine the ricotta and powdered ranch mix, and mix well.

4. In another bowl, combine the chicken and hot sauce, and mix to coat the chicken with the sauce.

5. Spread the ricotta mixture all over the prebaked crust, to within half an inch of the edges.

6. Arrange the chicken over the ricotta, and top with the mozzarella.

7. Bake for 6 to 10 more minutes, until the edges of the crust are golden brown and the cheese melts.

8. Top with fresh chives (if using), and serve with ranch dressing on the side (if using).

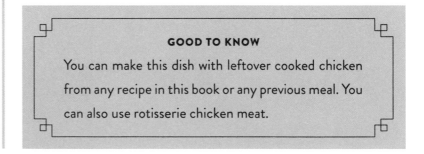

GOOD TO KNOW

You can make this dish with leftover cooked chicken from any recipe in this book or any previous meal. You can also use rotisserie chicken meat.

ALSO GOOD TO KNOW

Instead of a container of refrigerated pizza dough, you can use a 1-pound package of store-bought, fresh pizza dough or fresh dough from your favorite pizza restaurant.

Round One
Skillet Chicken *with* Sun-Dried Tomato Relish

A blender or food processor makes quick work of this unbelievable relish, and the result is a thick puree of sweet tomatoes, floral basil, grassy onions, tangy vinegar, and pungent garlic. The flavors are so robust, you need little else to transform ordinary chicken into something extraordinary.

This relish packs a sweet/tart flavor punch, so I encourage you to make extra to spoon over steak, potatoes, or pasta and to slather onto your sandwiches and paninis.

Serves 4, with leftover chicken for a future meal

10 to 15 minutes

15 minutes

½ cup fresh basil leaves, packed

½ cup oil-packed sun-dried tomatoes, drained, reserving 1 teaspoon oil from the jar

2 green onions, chopped

1 tablespoon red wine vinegar

2 to 3 cloves garlic, minced

½ teaspoon crushed red pepper flakes, or to taste

½ teaspoon dried oregano

Salt and freshly ground black pepper

2 tablespoons olive oil

8 boneless, skinless chicken breast halves, about 5 ounces each

All-purpose seasoning or salt and freshly ground black pepper

1. In a food processor or blender, combine the basil, sun-dried tomatoes and teaspoon of oil from the jar, green onions, red wine vinegar, garlic, red pepper flakes (if using), and oregano. Process until finely ground and blended, scraping down the sides of the bowl or blender as necessary. If the mixture seems too thick, add about 1 teaspoon of water, and process until you have a thick relish.

2. Transfer the relish to a bowl, and season with salt and black pepper. If you have the time, let stand for 20 minutes (and up to 24 hours; refrigerate if you're waiting longer than 2 hours).

3. Preheat the oven to 400°F. Line a large baking sheet with parchment paper or aluminum foil.

4. Heat the olive oil in a large skillet over medium-high heat. Season both sides of the chicken with all-purpose seasoning or salt and black pepper. Working in batches to prevent crowding the pan, add the chicken, and cook for 2 to 3 minutes per side, until golden brown.

5. Transfer the chicken to the prepared pan, and bake for 10 minutes, until the chicken is cooked through (a meat thermometer should register 165°F).

6. Reserve four of the chicken breasts for the Chicken Cheesesteaks with Fried Onions and Peppers (page 22) or another future meal. Refrigerate for up to 3 days.

7. Top the remaining chicken with the sun-dried tomato relish, and serve.

SERVING SUGGESTION: To round out the meal, serve the chicken with easy side dishes, such as steamed vegetables and roasted potatoes, or any easy side dish of choice. For more inspiration, check out Meal Prep 101 tips 23, 24, and 25.

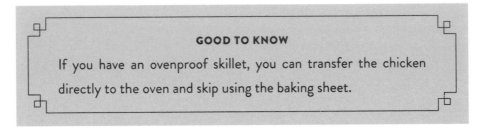

GOOD TO KNOW
If you have an ovenproof skillet, you can transfer the chicken directly to the oven and skip using the baking sheet.

Round Two

Chicken Cheesesteaks *with* Fried Onions *and* Peppers

Sometimes simple ingredient lists make for the best meals—not just because the preparation is easy but because with fewer competing flavors, each one has a chance to shine. In this dish, the onions and bell pepper are perfectly sweet and tender, and the chicken is enlivened with salty, tangy Worcestershire sauce. Choose your favorite rolls or carve up a baguette to complete this family favorite.

Serves 4

10 minutes

10 minutes

2 tablespoons olive oil, or vegetable oil, divided

1 large or 2 small yellow onions, sliced

1 bell pepper, any color, seeded and sliced

Salt and freshly ground black pepper

4 cups thinly sliced cooked chicken from the Skillet Chicken with Sun-Dried Tomato Relish (page 19), or any cooked chicken

1 tablespoon Worcestershire sauce

4 soft hoagie/sub rolls, or 1 baguette cut into 4 equal pieces, warmed if desired

1 cup cheddar, provolone, or cheese of choice, shredded or sliced

1. Heat 1 tablespoon of the olive oil (or vegetable oil) in a large skillet over medium-high heat. Add the onion and bell pepper, and cook for 3 to 5 minutes, until soft. Season the vegetables with salt and black pepper, and transfer to a plate. Cover with aluminum foil to keep warm.

2. Preheat the broiler. Heat the remaining oil in the same skillet over medium-high heat. Add the chicken and Worcestershire sauce, and cook for 2 to 3 minutes to heat through. Arrange the chicken in the hoagie rolls and top with the onions, peppers, and cheese. Place under the broiler to melt the cheese before serving, or serve as is.

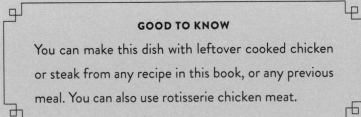

GOOD TO KNOW

You can make this dish with leftover cooked chicken or steak from any recipe in this book, or any previous meal. You can also use rotisserie chicken meat.

GOOD TO KNOW

If desired, you can make the meatballs with ground turkey or ground beef instead of chicken.

Chicken Meatballs
with Marsala Gravy

Just like chicken marsala but in meatball form. And since we're making meatballs instead of using the traditional chicken breasts or thighs, we can add a lot more flavor to the chicken. Each moist meatball is seasoned with parsley, onion, and garlic and then roasted to caramelized perfection. The gravy is a quick-and-easy, roux-based blend of chicken broth, cream, and sweet marsala. Not just great with these meatballs, the gravy is also excellent over baked chicken breasts and seared steaks.

Serves 4, with leftover meatballs for a future meal

10 minutes

20 to 25 minutes

2 pounds ground chicken

½ cup panko breadcrumbs

1 large egg

2 teaspoons dried parsley

1 teaspoon onion powder

½ teaspoon garlic powder

Salt and freshly ground
    black pepper

2 tablespoons unsalted butter

2 tablespoons all-purpose flour

1 cup chicken broth

½ cup marsala

½ cup heavy cream, or
    half-and-half

Chopped fresh parsley
    for serving

1. Preheat the oven to 400°F. Line a large baking sheet with parchment paper or aluminum foil.

2. In a large bowl, combine the chicken, breadcrumbs, egg, dried parsley, onion powder, garlic powder, 1 teaspoon salt, and ½ teaspoon black pepper. Mix well, and shape the mixture into 24 meatballs. Arrange the meatballs on the prepared pan, and bake for 18 to 20 minutes, until the meatballs are cooked through.

3. Reserve half (12) of the meatballs for the Chicken Meatball Soup (page 26) or another future meal. Refrigerate for up to 3 days.

4. Melt the butter in a large skillet over medium heat. When the butter is bubbling, whisk in the flour until blended. Whisk in the broth and marsala, and bring to a simmer. Simmer for 2 to 3 minutes, until the sauce thickens. Stir in the heavy cream (or half-and-half). Add the meatballs, and cook for 1 to 2 minutes to heat through.

5. Top with fresh parsley, and serve.

PREP AHEAD TIP: The meatballs can be assembled and refrigerated for up to 24 hours before baking.

SERVING SUGGESTION: Since this marsala sauce is so dreamy, I suggest you serve the meatballs and gravy over rice, pasta, or your favorite grain, and nestle a quick-and-easy raw or steamed vegetable on the side.

Round Two

Chicken Meatball Soup

Why should plain chicken have all the fun when chicken *meatballs* love to play in the soup pot too? And since these chicken meatballs are seasoned with parsley, onion, and garlic, they add great depth of flavor to this comforting soup (without any extra work on your part). Add some aromatic vegetables and tender egg noodles, and this ultra-healthy meal is complete. Plus, the egg noodles cook directly in the broth, so they absorb all the flavor from the very beginning. Every tender noodle and chunk of chicken meatball is brimming with flavor.

Serves 4

10 minutes

15 to 20 minutes

1 tablespoon olive oil

1 cup chopped carrots

1 cup chopped celery

½ cup chopped onion, any color

2 cloves garlic, minced

4 cups chicken broth

8 ounces wide or extra wide egg noodles

12 cooked meatballs from Chicken Meatballs with Marsala Gravy (page 25), quartered, or 2 cups cubed cooked chicken

½ cup frozen corn, kept frozen until ready to use

Grated parmesan cheese for serving

1. Heat the olive oil in a large stock pot or saucepan over medium-high heat. Add the carrots, celery, and onion, and cook for 3 to 5 minutes, until soft. Add the garlic, and cook for 30 seconds.

2. Add the broth, and bring to a simmer.

3. Add the egg noodles, and cook for 7 to 9 minutes, until the noodles are tender, stirring occasionally. Add the meatballs and corn, and cook for 2 to 3 minutes, until the meatballs are heated through. Season to taste with salt and black pepper.

4. Ladle the soup into bowls, and top with parmesan cheese.

Round One

One-Pot Barbecue Pulled Chicken

You will be amazed by the unbelievable amount of flavor you get from this one-pan meal. The chicken is cooked directly in a sweet, savory, and smoky sauce—a rich and thick medley made with pantry staples. Serve the pulled chicken on buns, rolls, soft tortillas, or lettuce leaves and the whole clan will be swooning.

Serves 4, with leftover chicken for a future meal

5 to 10 minutes

20 minutes

1 ½ cups chicken broth

1 ½ cups ketchup

1 tablespoon chili powder

1 tablespoon cider vinegar

1 tablespoon Worcestershire sauce

1 teaspoon dijon mustard

1 teaspoon garlic powder

1 teaspoon liquid smoke

1 teaspoon onion powder

Salt and freshly ground black pepper

2 ½ pounds boneless, skinless chicken breast halves, tenders, or thighs

Rolls, buns, or soft tortillas for serving

1. In a large stock pot or saucepan, whisk together the broth, ketchup, chili powder, cider vinegar, Worcestershire sauce, dijon mustard, garlic powder, liquid smoke, onion powder, 1 teaspoon salt, and ½ teaspoon black pepper. Add the chicken, set the pan over medium-high heat, and bring to a simmer. Reduce the heat to medium-low, partially cover, and simmer for 15 minutes, until you can easily shred the chicken with two forks.

2. Shred the chicken into the sauce.

3. Return the mixture to a simmer over medium-low heat, and simmer for 5 minutes, until the sauce thickens and reduces. Season to taste with salt and black pepper.

4. Reserve half of the chicken for the Mexican Chicken with Rice and Corn (page 30) or another future meal. Refrigerate for up to 3 days.

5. Serve the remaining chicken in rolls, buns, soft tortillas, or even lettuce cups.

Round Two
Mexican Chicken
with Rice *and* Corn

This isn't your average chicken and rice, and that's because one ingredient changes the game—enchilada sauce. Red enchilada sauce is a smooth, satiny sauce made from red chiles, tomatoes, and spices. Much richer than plain tomato sauce, it adds incredible depth to a variety of dishes. In this recipe, I used mild red enchilada sauce, but you can also use green enchilada sauce and choose between mild and hot.

Serves 4

5 to 10 minutes

15 to 20 minutes

2 cups red enchilada sauce, or tomato sauce

1 teaspoon chili powder

1 teaspoon dried cilantro

½ teaspoon ground cumin

Salt and freshly ground black pepper

2 ½ to 3 cups cubed or shredded cooked chicken from the One-Pot Barbecue Pulled Chicken (page 29), or any cooked chicken

2 cups cooked rice of choice

1 (11-ounce) can fiesta-style corn (corn with red and green bell peppers), drained

1 cup shredded Mexican cheese blend, or a blend of cheddar and Monterey jack, divided

Chopped green onions for serving

1. In a large skillet, whisk together the enchilada sauce (or tomato sauce), chili powder, cilantro, cumin, ½ teaspoon salt, and ¼ teaspoon black pepper. Set the pan over medium heat, and bring to a simmer. Reduce the heat to medium-low, and simmer for 10 minutes.

2. Add the chicken and simmer for 5 minutes.

3. Fold in the rice, corn, and ½ cup of the cheese, and cook for 1 to 2 minutes to heat through and melt the cheese.

4. Top with the remaining cheese and green onions, and serve.

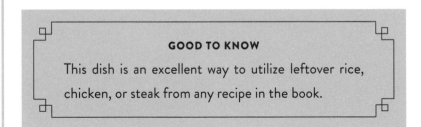

GOOD TO KNOW

This dish is an excellent way to utilize leftover rice, chicken, or steak from any recipe in the book.

GOOD TO KNOW

Feel free to add your favorite vegetables to the sheet pan. Since the chicken cooks for 25 minutes, you can add longer-cooking vegetables, such as potatoes, sweet potatoes, and carrots. Cut the vegetables into small pieces, toss with olive oil, season with salt and black pepper, and add them to the pan when you add the chicken.

Sheet Pan Honey-Balsamic Chicken

This undeniably appetizing, colorful (and customizable) meal is made in one pan and is ready in a flash. The chicken is glazed with a quick-and-easy marinade of tangy balsamic vinegar, garlic, dijon mustard, and sweet honey. The sweet/savory glaze is reminiscent of a lively vinaigrette with hints of oregano and thyme. As the chicken bakes, sweet red onion and fresh tomatoes soften and caramelize alongside it.

Serves 4, with leftover chicken for a future meal

5 minutes

25 minutes

¼ cup balsamic vinegar

3 tablespoons olive oil

2 tablespoons honey

2 cloves garlic, minced

1 teaspoon dijon mustard

1 teaspoon dried oregano

1 teaspoon dried thyme

Salt and freshly ground black pepper

8 boneless, skinless chicken breast halves, or 16 boneless, skinless thighs, patted dry

½ large red onion, cut into wedges

1 cup cherry or grape tomatoes

Chopped fresh basil or parsley for serving

1. In a large shallow dish, whisk together the balsamic vinegar, olive oil, honey, garlic, dijon mustard, oregano, thyme, ½ teaspoon salt, and ¼ teaspoon black pepper. Add the chicken, and turn to coat, pressing the marinade into the meat. If you have the time, marinate for 30 minutes or up to 24 hours in the refrigerator.

2. Preheat the oven to 400°F. Line a large baking sheet with parchment paper or aluminum foil.

3. Remove the chicken from the marinade, discard the marinade, and transfer the chicken to the prepared pan.

4. Arrange the onions all around the chicken on the baking sheet. Bake for 15 minutes. Arrange the tomatoes around the chicken and onions, and bake for 10 more minutes, until the chicken is cooked through (a meat thermometer should register 165°F for all cuts of chicken).

5. Reserve half of the chicken for the Chicken and Apple Salad with Fennel (page 34) or another future meal. Refrigerate for up to 3 days.

6. Serve the remaining chicken with the onions and tomatoes, topped with fresh basil or parsley.

Round Two

Chicken *and* Apple Salad *with* Fennel

This salad is bright, fresh, creamy, crisp, and packed with flavor. I love how it's *just creamy enough* but not so much that you can't taste each individual ingredient. The apples partner perfectly with the anise essence of the fennel and the sweet, feathery dill. Any apple variety works, so you can choose your favorite (tart or sweet, or a combination).

Serves 4

10 to 15 minutes

⅔ cup mayonnaise

2 tablespoons chopped fresh
   dill, or ½ teaspoon dried

1 tablespoon olive oil

1 teaspoon dijon mustard

4 cups cubed cooked chicken
   from the Sheet Pan
   Honey-Balsamic
   Chicken (page 33), or
   any cooked chicken

1 apple (such as Mackintosh,
   Honeycrisp, or Jonagold),
   cored and cubed

1 cup chopped celery

1 cup chopped fennel, plus
   fennel fronds for garnish

Salt and freshly ground
   black pepper

1. In a large bowl, whisk together the mayonnaise, dill, olive oil, and dijon mustard. Fold in the chicken, apple, celery, and fennel. Season to taste with salt and black pepper. Garnish with fennel fronds, and serve.

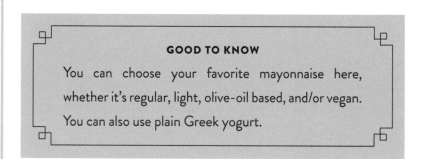

GOOD TO KNOW

You can choose your favorite mayonnaise here, whether it's regular, light, olive-oil based, and/or vegan. You can also use plain Greek yogurt.

GOOD TO KNOW

The leftover chicken from this meal works beautifully in all the Round Two recipes in this book.

Round One

Sheet Pan Parsley Lemon Chicken

Fresh and light, this tender chicken is scented with tangy lemon, garlic, parsley, and a hint of dijon mustard. And although it's made in a flash with pantry staples, flavors soar with every juicy bite.

🍴 Serves 4, with leftover chicken for a future meal

🥄 5 minutes

🔥 25 to 30 minutes

3 tablespoons olive oil

1 ½ teaspoons dijon mustard

1 ½ teaspoons dried parsley

3 to 4 cloves garlic, minced

8 boneless, skinless chicken breast halves

2 bell peppers, any color, seeded and cut into 2-inch pieces, or 2 cups chopped mini peppers

Salt and freshly ground black pepper

1 lemon, cut into wedges or slices

Chopped fresh parsley for serving, optional

1. Preheat the oven to 400°F. Line a large baking sheet with parchment paper or aluminum foil.

2. In a shallow dish, whisk together the olive oil, dijon mustard, dried parsley, and garlic. Add the chicken and bell peppers, and toss to coat. If you have the time, marinate for 30 minutes or up to 24 hours in the refrigerator.

3. Arrange the chicken and peppers on the prepared pan. Season with salt and black pepper. Arrange the lemon wedges/slices alongside.

4. Bake for 25 to 30 minutes, until the chicken is cooked through (a meat thermometer should register 165°F).

5. Reserve 3 to 4 chicken breasts for the Sweet-and-Sour Chicken with Rice Noodles (page 38) or another future meal. Refrigerate for up to 3 days.

6. Top the remaining chicken with fresh parsley (if using), and serve.

PREP AHEAD TIP: If you want to prep the chicken in advance, combine it with the bell pepper and olive oil mixture and refrigerate for up to 24 hours. For easy cleanup, marinate the chicken in freezer bags.

SERVING SUGGESTION: For a complete and filling meal, serve the chicken with your favorite raw or steamed vegetable and a starchy side, such as rice, beans, pasta, potatoes, sweet potatoes, quinoa, couscous, or whole grain bread. For more inspiration, check out my Meal Prep 101 tips 23, 24, and 25.

Round Two

Sweet-and-Sour Chicken *with* Rice Noodles

This slick, shimmering sauce boasts equal parts sweetness and saltiness, flavors that catapult the chicken and noodles to new flavor heights. Traditional sweet-and-sour sauce often contains brown sugar, but I chose to use apricot preserves instead—the fruity jam not only adds sweetness, it adds little nuggets of chewy-sweet apricot. You can't get *that* from brown sugar. Don't have apricot preserves? No problem. Orange marmalade works too.

Serves 4

10 minutes

10 minutes

12 ounces rice noodles, also called pad thai noodles

2 cups sugar snap peas, ends trimmed

2 cups apricot preserves, or orange marmalade

3 tablespoons soy sauce

1 tablespoon mirin (Japanese rice wine)

1 teaspoon sesame oil

4 cups cubed cooked chicken from the Sheet Pan Parsley Lemon Chicken (page 37), or any cooked chicken

2 tablespoons chopped fresh cilantro

Salt and freshly ground black pepper

1. Cook the noodles in a large pot of boiling water for 4 minutes, adding the sugar snap peas for the last minute of cooking. Drain and set aside.

2. Meanwhile, in a large skillet or saucepan, combine the apricot preserves (or orange marmalade), soy sauce, mirin, and sesame oil. Set the pan over medium heat, and bring to a simmer.

3. Add the chicken and cook for 1 to 2 minutes to heat through. Fold in the noodles, sugar snap peas, and fresh cilantro.

4. Season to taste with salt and black pepper, and serve.

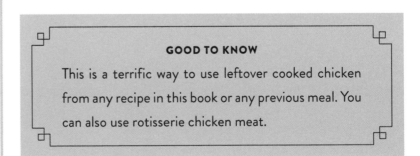

GOOD TO KNOW

This is a terrific way to use leftover cooked chicken from any recipe in this book or any previous meal. You can also use rotisserie chicken meat.

Baked Buttermilk Fried Chicken

Crispy on the outside and moist on the inside, this baked chicken tastes exactly like its fried counterpart, but it has a fraction of the calories and fat. And the buttermilk serves a purpose beyond adding sweet tang to the chicken; the acidic dairy marinates and tenderizes the meat in just minutes. The buttermilk also works well with the other flavors in the dish—namely the ranch dip mix!

Serves 4, with leftover chicken for a future meal

10 minutes

20 minutes

8 boneless, skinless chicken breast halves

1 ½ cups all-purpose flour

Salt and freshly ground black pepper

2 cups buttermilk

¼ cup or 2 (1-ounce) packets powdered ranch dip/ dressing mix

1 large egg

3 cups panko breadcrumbs

2 tablespoons unsalted butter, cut into ¼-inch pieces

Chopped fresh parsley for serving, optional

1. Preheat the oven to 400°F. Line a large baking sheet with parchment paper or aluminum foil.

2. Place the chicken in large freezer bags or between two pieces of plastic wrap, and pound to 1 ½-inch thickness. Set aside.

3. Place the flour in a shallow dish, and season it with salt and black pepper.

4. In a second shallow dish, whisk together the buttermilk, ranch mix, and egg.

5. Place the panko breadcrumbs in a third shallow dish.

6. Add the chicken to the flour, and turn to coat. Shake off excess flour, and transfer the chicken to the buttermilk mixture. Turn to coat, shake off excess buttermilk mixture, and transfer the chicken to the breadcrumbs. Turn to coat.

7. Transfer the chicken to the prepared pan, and top with the butter pieces.

8. Bake for 25 to 30 minutes, until the chicken is cooked through (a meat thermometer should register 165°F) and the crust is crisp and golden. Season the top of the chicken with salt and black pepper.

9. Reserve 3 to 4 chicken breasts for the Chicken Tetrazzini with Mushrooms and Peas (page 42) or another future meal. Refrigerate for up to 3 days.

10. Top the remaining chicken with fresh parsley (if using), and serve.

Round Two

Chicken Tetrazzini *with* Mushrooms *and* Peas

Quite possibly the best chicken tetrazzini ever. Why? It's the breaded chicken from the Baked Buttermilk Fried Chicken (page 41) that makes all the difference. Most tetrazzini recipes start with a butter-flour roux, which works as a thickener for the cream sauce. Since the chicken is already coated with seasoned flour and panko breadcrumbs, you don't need the flour, *and* you get added flavor from the ranch seasoning.

Serves 4

10 to 15 minutes

15 minutes

8 ounces egg noodles

2 tablespoons unsalted butter

4 ounces button or cremini
    mushrooms, sliced

¾ teaspoon onion powder

½ teaspoon garlic powder

½ teaspoon dried thyme

Salt and freshly ground
    black pepper

1 cup half-and-half, or milk

1 teaspoon dijon mustard

3 cups cubed chicken from
    the Baked Buttermilk
    Fried Chicken (page 41),
    or any cooked chicken

½ cup frozen green peas, kept
    frozen until ready to use

½ cup shredded cheddar cheese

½ cup shredded mozzarella
    cheese

2 tablespoons chopped fresh
    parsley, optional

1. Cook the egg noodles according to the package directions. Drain, and cover with aluminum foil to keep warm.

2. Meanwhile, melt the butter in a large skillet or saucepan over medium heat. Add the mushrooms, and cook for 5 minutes, until soft. Add the onion powder, garlic powder, thyme, ½ teaspoon salt, and ¼ teaspoon black pepper, and stir to coat. Cook for 30 seconds, until the thyme is fragrant. Add the half-and-half (or milk) and dijon mustard, and bring to a simmer.

3. Add the chicken, reduce the heat to low, partially cover, and simmer for 10 minutes.

4. Fold in the cooked noodles and peas, and cook for 1 minute to heat through. Season to taste with salt and black pepper.

5. Top with the cheddar and mozzarella cheeses, cover the pan with aluminum foil or a lid, and remove it from the heat. Let stand for 1 minute to melt the cheese.

6. Top with fresh parsley (if using), and serve.

GOOD TO KNOW

If you don't have leftover breaded chicken, simply add 1 tablespoon of all-purpose flour to the pan when you add the onion powder, garlic powder, and thyme.

ALSO GOOD TO KNOW

This recipe works with any leftover chicken and (more traditionally) with cooked turkey.

GOOD TO KNOW

Hoisin sauce is sold in the Asian food
aisle of the grocery store.

Sweet Sriracha Chicken
with Mini Peppers

It's not often you see the words *sweet* and *sriracha* in the same sentence, but their pairing makes for a brilliant sauce. In this recipe, sweet hoisin sauce—made with fermented soybeans, sugar, and spices—is coupled with fiery sriracha sauce to create a tantalizing glaze for chicken, peppers, and onions. The sauce is glossy and satiny and delivers the ideal balance of heat and sweet.

Serves 4, with leftover chicken for a future meal

10 to 15 minutes

15 to 20 minutes

2 tablespoons peanut oil, divided

2 pounds boneless, skinless chicken breast halves, cut into bite-size pieces

Salt and freshly ground black pepper

2 cups sliced sweet mini peppers, or 1 bell pepper, any color, seeded and sliced into thin strips

1 large or 2 small onions, any color, chopped

½ cup chicken broth, or water

½ cup hoisin sauce

2 tablespoons sriracha sauce, or chili garlic sauce, plus more for serving

1. Heat 1 tablespoon of the peanut oil in a large skillet over medium-high heat. Add the chicken, and cook until golden brown on all sides, stirring frequently. Season the chicken with salt and black pepper. Transfer the chicken to a plate and set aside.

2. Heat the remaining oil in the same pan over medium-high heat. Add the peppers and onions, and cook for 3 to 5 minutes, until soft.

3. Add the broth (or water), hoisin sauce, and sriracha sauce, and bring to a simmer.

4. Return the chicken to the pan with any accumulated juices from the plate. Reduce the heat to low, and simmer for 5 to 7 minutes, until the chicken is cooked through and the sauce thickens.

5. Reserve half of the chicken for the Chicken Tortilla Soup (page 46) or another future meal. Refrigerate for up to 3 days.

6. Top the remaining chicken with fresh cilantro, and serve.

SERVING SUGGESTION: This is a "saucy" dish, and you won't want to miss a drop of it, so I suggest serving the chicken and peppers over rice, couscous, quinoa, or your favorite grain.

Round Two
Chicken Tortilla Soup

You will adore the multiple layers of flavor and texture in this one pot soup. The savory broth is seasoned with chili, cilantro, and cumin and studded with chunks of chicken, corn, and tomatoes. Then, sharp, stretchy Mexican cheese and crisp tortilla chips round out the soup, adding more layers of taste and textural enjoyment for the palate.

Serves 4

10 to 15 minutes

10 minutes

2 (15-ounce) cans fire-
    roasted diced tomatoes

2 cups chicken broth

2 cups cubed cooked chicken
    from the Sweet Sriracha
    Chicken with Mini
    Peppers (page 45), or
    any cooked chicken

1 cup fresh, frozen, or canned
    corn of any type
    (including fiesta-style
    corn with bell peppers)

1 ½ teaspoons chili powder,
    regular or hot

1 teaspoon dried cilantro

½ teaspoon ground cumin

Salt and freshly ground
    black pepper

Tortilla chips for serving

Shredded Mexican cheese
    for serving, or a blend of
    cheddar and monterey jack

Chopped green onions
    for serving

Fresh cilantro leaves for serving

1. In a large stock pot or saucepan, combine the tomatoes, broth, chicken, corn, chili powder, dried cilantro, and cumin. Set the pan over medium-high heat, and bring to a simmer.

2. Reduce the heat to medium-low, and simmer for 10 minutes. Season to taste with salt and black pepper.

3. Ladle the soup into bowls, and top with the tortilla chips, cheese, green onions, and fresh cilantro.

> **GOOD TO KNOW**
>
> This soup is easily customizable, so feel free to have some fun. For a hot/spicy version, add hot sauce or use hot chili powder. You can also add beans—regular canned beans, seasoned black beans, or seasoned chili beans of choice.

Paprika Chicken

Shortest ingredient list—biggest flavor! This is the perfect meal for a busy weeknight; it's quick, easy, and the oven does all the work. You need just three ingredients—butter, garlic, and paprika—to transform chicken thighs into a juicy, savory, finger-licking meal.

Serves 4, with leftover chicken for a future meal

5 minutes

25 minutes

16 bone-in chicken thighs, 4 ½ to 5 pounds, patted dry

Salt and freshly ground black pepper

5 tablespoons unsalted butter, melted

1 ½ teaspoons garlic powder, or granulated garlic

1 teaspoon paprika

Chopped fresh parsley or basil for serving, optional

1. Preheat the oven to 400°F. Coat a shallow baking dish with cooking spray or a thin layer of olive oil.

2. Season both sides of the chicken thighs with salt and black pepper, and transfer them to the prepared pan, skin side up.

3. In a small bowl, whisk together the butter, garlic, and paprika. Brush the mixture all over the top and sides of the chicken thighs.

4. Bake for 25 to 30 minutes, until a meat thermometer registers 165°F when inserted into the thickest part.

5. Reserve half of the chicken thighs for the Green Chicken Enchiladas (page 50) or another future meal. Refrigerate for up to 3 days.

6. Top the remaining chicken thighs with fresh parsley or basil (if using), and serve.

SERVING SUGGESTION: For a complete meal, serve the chicken thighs with your favorite raw or steamed vegetable and a starchy side, such as rice, beans, pasta, potatoes, sweet potatoes, quinoa, couscous, or whole grain bread. For more inspiration, check out my Meal Prep 101 tips 23, 24, and 25.

Round Two
Green Chicken Enchiladas

Soft flour tortillas, overflowing with chicken, cheese, seasoned beans, and green chilies. These nourishing bundles are nestled in a baking dish and topped with enchilada sauce and more cheese. Hearty, comforting, and not only perfect for a busy weeknight, this dish is also great for entertaining.

Serves 4

10 minutes

20 minutes

4 cups shredded cooked chicken from the Paprika Chicken (page 49), or any cooked chicken

3 cups shredded Mexican cheese blend, divided

1 (15-ounce) can seasoned black beans or chili beans of choice, undrained

1 (4-ounce) can diced green chiles

1 teaspoon chili powder

8 soft taco-size flour tortillas

1 (28-ounce) can green enchilada sauce

Chopped fresh cilantro for serving

Chopped green onions for serving

1. Preheat the oven to 350°F. Coat a 9-by-13-inch baking dish with cooking spray.

2. In a large bowl, combine the chicken, 1 ½ cups of the cheese, beans, green chiles, and chili powder. Mix well.

3. Arrange the tortillas on a flat surface. Top the center of each tortilla with about 2 tablespoons of the enchilada sauce, making a line down the center. Top the sauce with the chicken mixture, about ½ cup, filling up the center, from one end of the tortilla to the other.

4. Roll up tightly, and arrange the filled tortillas in the prepared pan (seam side up or down, it doesn't matter; just pack them in tightly). Top the tortillas with the remaining enchilada sauce (if it seems like you have too much sauce for your pan, leave about ½ cup out). Top with the remaining cheese.

5. Cover with aluminum foil (spray the aluminum foil with cooking spray to prevent sticking), and bake for 15 minutes. Uncover and bake for 5 more minutes, until the cheese melts and the tortillas are golden and crisp where they're not covered with sauce and/or cheese.

6. Top with fresh cilantro and green onions, and serve.

SERVING SUGGESTION: You can top these enchiladas with additional ingredients if desired; sour cream, avocado, jalapeños, salsa, and black olives would all make great garnishes.

GOOD TO KNOW

Green enchilada sauce is a blend of green chiles, green tomatoes, and jalapeños, and it's a one-stop shop for great flavor. Look for the sauce (typically sold in cans) in the Mexican food aisle of the grocery store. If desired, you can use red enchilada sauce instead.

ALSO GOOD TO KNOW

Since this recipe calls for seasoned beans, you need very few additional ingredients. You can use seasoned black beans or chili beans of choice. If you don't have seasoned beans, you can certainly use regular canned beans; just rinse and drain them before using to remove excess salt.

Round One

White Wine–Braised Chicken Thighs *with* Artichokes *and* Olives

Pan-seared to lock in flavor, this chicken is scented with paprika, oregano, and onion and simmered in a wine-infused sauce with briny artichokes and olives. This hearty, one-skillet meal is great for any busy weeknight and fancy enough to serve at your next dinner party.

Serves 4, with leftover chicken for a future meal

10 minutes

20 minutes

4 ½ to 5 pounds bone-in, skinless chicken thighs, patted dry
Salt and freshly ground black pepper
½ cup all-purpose flour
1 teaspoon dried oregano
1 teaspoon paprika
½ teaspoon onion powder
3 tablespoons olive oil
1 cup white wine, or chicken broth
1 (14-ounce) can artichoke hearts, drained and quartered
½ cup pimento-stuffed green olives
Chopped fresh parsley for serving

1. Season the chicken all over with salt and black pepper.
2. In a shallow dish or large zip-top bag, combine the flour, oregano, paprika, and onion powder. Add the chicken, and turn to coat both sides. Shake off excess flour.
3. Heat the olive oil in a large, high-sided skillet over medium-high heat. Working in batches to prevent crowding the pan, add the chicken and cook for 3 to 5 minutes, until golden brown on both sides. Transfer the chicken to a plate, leaving any browned bits in the bottom of the pan.
4. Reduce the heat to medium, and add the wine to the skillet. Bring to a simmer, scraping up any browned bits from the bottom of the pan and incorporating them into the sauce. Add the artichokes and olives, and return to a simmer. Return the chicken to the pan with any accumulated juices from the plate.
5. Reduce the heat to medium-low, partially cover, and simmer for 10 to 12 minutes, until the chicken is cooked through (a meat thermometer should register 165°F when inserted into the thickest part).
6. Remove the lid, and simmer until the sauce thickens slightly, about 1 to 2 minutes.

7. Reserve half of the chicken for the Chicken Tamale Pie (page 56) or another future meal. Refrigerate for up to 3 days.

8. Top the remaining chicken with fresh parsley, and serve.

ALSO GOOD TO KNOW

The artichoke hearts used in this recipe are the canned variety, which are sold whole, halved, or quartered and packed in brine. You can save a step by purchasing the quartered artichoke hearts. You can also use marinated artichoke hearts; they're just slightly more expensive.

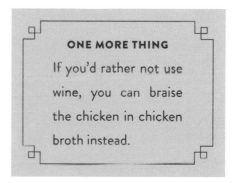

ONE MORE THING

If you'd rather not use wine, you can braise the chicken in chicken broth instead.

Round Two
Chicken Tamale Pie

Like deconstructed tamales, this dish boasts a bottom layer of taco-seasoned cornbread and a top layer of chicken, corn, enchilada sauce, and cheese. And the best part (and perhaps the most fun part) is the holes we poke in the cornbread. Just like a poke cake, the holes allow the chicken mixture and enchilada sauce to weave in and out of the cornbread, adding flavor and keeping each bite moist and delectable.

Serves 4

5 to 10 minutes

17 to 20 minutes

1 (8.5-ounce) box corn muffin mix (such as Jiffy)

⅓ cup milk

2 tablespoons unsalted butter, melted

1 large egg

2 teaspoons taco seasoning

½ cup corn, canned, fresh, or frozen, thawed if frozen

2 cups shredded cooked chicken from the White Wine–Braised Chicken Thighs with Artichokes and Olives (page 53), or any cooked chicken

1 cup red enchilada sauce, divided

1 cup shredded monterey jack cheese, or a blend of cheddar and jack, or Mexican cheese blend

Fresh cilantro leaves (whole or chopped) for serving

1. Preheat the oven to 400°F. Coat a 9-inch pie plate or oven-safe skillet (such as cast iron) with cooking spray.

2. In a large bowl, whisk together the corn muffin mix, milk, butter, egg, and taco seasoning. Fold in the corn. Transfer the mixture to the prepared pan, and smooth the surface. Bake for 12 to 15 minutes, until a wooden pick inserted near the center comes out clean or with moist bits clinging to it.

3. Meanwhile, in a large skillet or saucepan, combine the chicken and ¾ cup of the enchilada sauce. Set the pan over medium heat and warm the mixture through.

4. Using the end of a wooden spoon or spatula, poke holes all over the cornbread in the pan. Pour the remaining enchilada sauce into the holes. Top the cornbread with the chicken mixture. Top with the cheese.

5. Bake for 5 minutes, until the cheese melts.

6. Top with fresh cilantro, and serve.

GOOD TO KNOW

This dish works with leftover chicken from any recipe in this book or any previous meal. You can also use rotisserie chicken meat.

GOOD TO KNOW

To save time, feel free to use your favorite store-bought marinara sauce or pasta sauce instead of making the sauce from scratch. Keep in mind, using store-bought marinara is efficient, but it can get costly. And that's assuming your favorite brand is on the shelf. Bookmark my go-to marinara sauce below, whether you make it today or not. It's made with pantry staples, ultra-inexpensive, and a good thing to keep on hand for days when you need a fast, delicious marinara sauce.

ALSO GOOD TO KNOW

This is an excellent, gluten-free way to make chicken fingers for a crowd.

Round One
Parmesan Chicken Fingers *with* Marinara

Chicken fingers elevated! Baked, not fried, these cheesy chicken fingers are laced with butter and then coated with garlic and parmesan cheese. After a quick trip to the oven, the inside of each chicken finger is moist and tender, and the outside is crisp and golden brown. It's impossible to stop eating them.

Serves 4, with leftover chicken for a future meal

15 minutes

15 minutes

FOR THE CHICKEN FINGERS:

4 tablespoons unsalted butter

2 cloves garlic, smashed

2 pounds chicken tenders, patted dry (don't skip this step; it helps the butter and coating stick)

1 cup grated parmesan cheese

Salt and freshly ground black pepper

FOR THE MARINARA SAUCE:

1 ½ cups tomato sauce

2 tablespoons granulated sugar

1 teaspoon dried basil

1 teaspoon dried oregano

½ teaspoon garlic powder

½ teaspoon onion powder

1. Preheat the oven to 400°F. Line a large baking sheet with parchment paper or aluminum foil.

2. To prepare the chicken, combine the butter and garlic in a medium saucepan, and set the pan over medium heat. Cook until the butter is melted and bubbling. Remove the pan from the heat.

3. Add the chicken tenders to the butter, and turn to coat.

4. In a shallow dish, combine the parmesan cheese, ½ teaspoon salt, and ¼ teaspoon black pepper. Add the chicken tenders to the cheese, and turn to coat, pressing the cheese into the meat. Transfer the tenders to the prepared pan, and bake for 15 to 20 minutes, until golden brown and cooked through (a meat thermometer should register 165°F).

5. Meanwhile, to make the marinara sauce, combine all ingredients in a medium saucepan, and set the pan over medium heat. Bring to a simmer, reduce the heat to medium-low, and cook for 10 minutes. Season to taste with salt and black pepper.

6. Reserve about one quarter of the chicken tenders for the Chicken Macaroni and Cheese (page 60) or another future meal. Refrigerate for up to 3 days.

7. Serve the remaining chicken tenders with the marinara sauce on the side for dunking.

Chicken Macaroni *and* Cheese

This macaroni and cheese will rock your world. The pasta is perfectly tender, and the cheese sauce is buttery, sharp, and stretchy. The sauce is also scented with onion and garlic, so you get layer upon layer of flavor in every creamy bite. Plus, adding chicken not only ramps up protein, but it also adds another level of flavor and texture.

Serves 4

10 minutes

15 minutes

12 ounces elbow macaroni

4 tablespoons unsalted butter

4 tablespoons all-purpose flour

2 ½ cups milk, or half-and-half

1 teaspoon garlic powder

1 teaspoon onion powder

Salt and ground black pepper

1 ½ cups shredded sharp
    cheddar cheese

1 cup shredded mozzarella
    cheese

2 cups cubed cooked chicken
    from the Parmesan
    Chicken Fingers with
    Marinara (page 59), or
    any cooked chicken

Chopped fresh chives for
    serving, optional

1. Cook the pasta according to package directions. Drain, and cover with aluminum foil to keep warm.

2. Melt the butter in a large saucepan or high-sided skillet over medium heat. When the butter is bubbling, whisk in the flour until blended.

3. Gradually whisk in the milk (or half-and-half), and bring to a simmer. Whisk in the garlic powder, onion powder, ½ teaspoon salt, and ¼ teaspoon black pepper. Simmer for 2 minutes, until the mixture thickens, whisking frequently.

4. Reduce the heat to low, and stir in the cheddar and mozzarella cheeses.

5. Once the cheese has melted, fold in the pasta and chicken. Cook for 1 minute to heat through.

6. Remove the pan from the heat, and season to taste with salt and black pepper. Top with fresh chives (if using), and serve.

Round One
Sheet Pan Chicken Shawarma

Warm, smoky, earthy, and topped with a splash of lemon, this chicken is as comforting as it is tantalizing. The vibrant spices deliver a tremendous amount of flavor as they bake into the chicken (plus, they are all staples of the spice rack). These traditional warming flavors pair beautifully with the cool, cumin-scented yogurt.

Serves 4, with leftover chicken for a future meal

5 to 10 minutes

25 to 30 minutes

FOR THE CHICKEN:

3 tablespoons olive oil, divided

1 tablespoon fresh lemon juice

3 cloves garlic, minced

2 teaspoons ground cumin

1 teaspoon ground coriander

1 teaspoon smoked paprika

½ teaspoon cardamom

Salt and freshly ground
     black pepper

16 bone-in, skinless chicken
     thighs, about 4 ½ to 5
     pounds, patted dry

1 bell pepper, any color,
     seeded and sliced

2 to 3 green onions, cut
     into 2-inch pieces

FOR THE YOGURT SAUCE:

1 cup plain Greek yogurt

1 teaspoon ground cumin

½ teaspoon garlic powder or
     minced dried garlic

Squeeze of fresh lemon

1. To prepare the chicken, in a large resealable bag or container with a lid, combine 2 tablespoons of the olive oil, lemon juice, garlic, cumin, coriander, paprika, cardamom, ½ teaspoon salt, and ¼ teaspoon black pepper. Add the chicken, and turn to coat. For the best results, massage the marinade into the chicken. If you have the time, marinate for 30 minutes or up to 24 hours in the refrigerator.

2. Preheat the oven to 400°F. Line a large baking sheet with parchment paper or aluminum foil.

3. Remove the chicken from the marinade, discard the marinade, and transfer the chicken to the prepared pan. Bake for 20 minutes.

4. Meanwhile, toss the bell pepper slices and green onions with the remaining olive oil, and season with salt and pepper.

5. Once the chicken has cooked for 20 minutes, arrange the pepper slices and onions around the chicken on the baking sheet. Return the pan to the oven and bake for 5 to 10 more minutes, until the chicken is cooked through (a meat thermometer should register 165°F when inserted into the thickest part).

6. To make the yogurt sauce, combine all ingredients in a medium bowl, and mix well. Season to taste with salt and black pepper.

7. Reserve about one third of the chicken for the Creamy Chicken and Peas (page 66) or another future meal. Refrigerate for up to 3 days.

8. Serve the remaining chicken with the bell peppers, onions, and yogurt sauce.

SERVING SUGGESTION: Since shawarma is typically served as a sandwich, I suggest serving the chicken and vegetables in warm pita bread. Serve the yogurt sauce on the side for dunking.

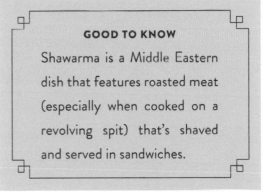

Creamy Chicken *and* Peas

Tender chunks of chicken, simmered in an aromatic, creamy, tomato-based sauce with sweet peas and nutty parmesan cheese. This is the ultimate go-to recipe for any busy weeknight. It's gluten-free and a true family favorite.

Serves 4

10 minutes

20 minutes

1 tablespoon olive oil

½ cup chopped onion, any color

2 cloves garlic, minced

1 ½ to 2 cups tomato sauce

1 teaspoon dried basil

2 cups cubed cooked chicken from the Sheet Pan Chicken Shawarma (page 63), or any cooked chicken

½ cup heavy cream, or half-and-half

½ cup frozen peas, kept frozen until ready to use

Salt and freshly ground black pepper

Grated parmesan cheese for serving, optional

1. Heat the olive oil in a large saucepan or skillet over medium-high heat. Add the onion, and cook for 3 to 5 minutes, until soft. Add the garlic, and cook for 30 seconds.

2. Add the tomato sauce and basil, and bring to a simmer. Add the chicken, and return to a simmer. Reduce the heat to medium-low, and cook for 10 minutes.

3. Stir in the heavy cream (or half-and-half) and peas, and simmer for 2 minutes to heat through. Season to taste with salt and black pepper. Top with parmesan cheese (if using), and serve.

GOOD TO KNOW

This dish is wholly satisfying on its own, but if you would like to stretch the meal, serve the chicken and sauce over pasta, rice, or your favorite grain.

This dish is Italian inspired, but the recipe can easily be transitioned by adding Mexican, Greek, and/or Indian seasonings. For Mexican flair, use a Mexican spice blend (instead of basil), and finish the dish with cotija or queso fresco cheese. For a Greek dish, use a Greek blend of herbs (to replace the basil), and top the dish with feta before serving. For an Indian-inspired dish, replace the basil with curry powder and cumin, and serve with a dollop of sour cream or yogurt.

Round One
Indian Butter Chicken

This classic dish delivers moist nuggets of chicken in a satiny, creamy sauce that asserts the warming essence of Indian spices. You'll be amazed by how much deep flavor evolves (in just minutes) with a few flavor-packed seasonings from your spice rack.

Serves 4, with leftover chicken for a future meal

10 to 15 minutes

20 minutes

1 tablespoon olive oil

½ cup chopped onion, any color

2 cloves garlic, minced

1 teaspoon grated fresh ginger

2 pounds boneless, skinless chicken breast halves, tenders, or thighs, cut into bite-size pieces

2 teaspoons chili powder

2 teaspoons garam masala

1 teaspoon ground cumin

1 teaspoon turmeric

Salt and freshly ground black pepper

1 cup chicken broth

3 tablespoons unsalted butter

2 tablespoons tomato paste

½ cup heavy cream

Chopped fresh cilantro for serving, optional

1. Heat the olive oil in a large skillet over medium-high heat. Add the onion, and cook for 3 to 5 minutes, until soft. Add the garlic and ginger, and cook for 30 seconds. Add the chicken, and cook until golden on all sides. Add the chili powder, garam masala, cumin, turmeric, ½ teaspoon salt, and ¼ teaspoon black pepper, and stir to coat. Cook for 1 minute, until the spices are fragrant.

2. Add the broth, butter, and tomato paste, and bring to a simmer. Reduce the heat to low, cover, and cook for 10 to 15 minutes, until chicken is cooked through.

3. Stir in the heavy cream, and cook until heated through, about 1 to 2 minutes.

4. Reserve half of the chicken for the Coconut Chicken Soup (page 70) or another future meal. Refrigerate for up to 3 days.

5. Top the remaining chicken with fresh cilantro (if using), and serve.

SERVING SUGGESTION: Since this sauce is so rich and delicious, you won't want to miss a drop. I suggest you serve the chicken and sauce over rice and/or with naan or your favorite flatbread.

Coconut Chicken Soup

This satiny soup delivers the flavor spectrum in every creamy spoonful. There's the balance of tangy lemon and lime with sweet coconut, followed by the fiery quality of curry paste and chile pepper. And this dish is completely customizable, so you can make it as spicy as you desire by using more/less of the diced chile pepper.

Serves 4

10 minutes

15 to 20 minutes

4 cups chicken broth

1 small red or green jalapeño pepper, seeded and sliced, or 2 Thai chiles, halved and seeded

1 lemongrass stalk, smashed and cut into 2-inch pieces

2 teaspoons red Thai curry paste

4 cups canned coconut milk, not coconut cream

2 cups cubed cooked chicken from the Indian Butter Chicken (page 69), or any cooked chicken

8 ounces sliced button or cremini mushrooms

1 tablespoon fish sauce, plus more to taste

1 tablespoon coconut sugar or granulated sugar, plus more to taste

1 tablespoon fresh lime juice, plus more to taste

Chopped green onions for serving

Fresh cilantro leaves for serving

1. In a large stock pot or saucepan, combine the broth, jalapeño, lemongrass, and curry paste. Set the pan over medium-high heat, and bring to a simmer. Simmer for 10 minutes.

2. Using a slotted spoon or fine sieve, remove and discard the pepper slices and lemongrass. Add the coconut milk, chicken, and mushrooms to the pan, and return to a simmer. Simmer for 5 to 10 minutes.

3. Add the fish sauce, coconut sugar (or granulated sugar), and lime juice. Adjust the seasoning by adding more sugar, fish sauce, and/or lime juice as desired.

4. Ladle the soup into bowls, and top with the green onions and fresh cilantro.

Round One
Orange Chicken

Better than takeout, this easy-to-make orange chicken will amaze you. The chicken is moist, and the crunchy coating is a sweet/savory blend of orange juice, soy sauce, sesame oil, and garlic. The trick to perfectly moist and crispy orange chicken? Cornstarch in the coating! Once the chicken pieces are coated in egg, they're tossed in a blend of cornstarch and flour. It's the cornstarch that ensures a golden, crisp exterior and moist interior.

Serves 4, with leftover chicken for a future meal

10 minutes

10 to 15 minutes

FOR THE CHICKEN:

2 large eggs

1 tablespoon vegetable oil, plus more for frying

Salt and freshly ground black pepper

½ cup cornstarch

¼ cup all-purpose flour

2 pounds chicken tenders, or boneless, skinless chicken breast halves, cut into bite-size pieces

FOR THE ORANGE SAUCE:

¾ cup orange juice

3 tablespoons soy sauce

2 tablespoons light or dark brown sugar

2 tablespoons mirin (Japanese rice wine)

½ teaspoon garlic powder

½ teaspoon sesame oil

¼ cup water

1 tablespoon cornstarch

Chopped green onions for serving

1. In a shallow bowl, whisk together the eggs and 1 tablespoon of the vegetable oil. Season with salt and black pepper, and set aside.

2. In another shallow bowl, whisk together the cornstarch and flour.

3. Heat about ½-inch of vegetable oil in a high-sided skillet or wok over medium-high heat, until it reaches 350 to 375°F.

4. Dip the chicken in the egg mixture, and turn to coat. Transfer the chicken to the cornstarch mixture, and turn to coat. Shake off any excess cornstarch mixture.

5. Working in batches to prevent crowding the pan, add the chicken to the hot oil, and fry for 3 to 4 minutes, until golden brown and cooked through. Using a slotted spoon or tongs, transfer the chicken to paper towels to drain. Wipe out the excess oil from the pan.

6. To make the sauce, add the orange juice, soy sauce, brown sugar, mirin, garlic powder, and sesame oil to the same pan, and whisk until blended.

7. Set the pan over medium-high heat, and bring to a simmer. Return the chicken to the pan, and stir to coat.

8. In a small bowl, whisk together the water and cornstarch. Add the mixture to the pan, and cook for 1 minute, until the sauce thickens.

9. Reserve half of the chicken for the Thai Chicken Fried Rice with Basil (page 76) or another future meal. Refrigerate for up to 3 days.

10. Top the remaining chicken with green onions, and serve.

GOOD TO KNOW
To save prep time, cut the chicken with your kitchen shears/scissors.

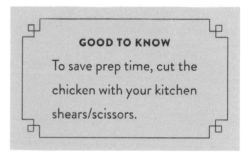

Round Two
Thai Chicken Fried Rice *with* Basil

Unlike traditional Chinese fried rice, this version asserts the unique flavor of fresh basil. Plus, we're using the leftover Orange Chicken (page 73), and the orange essence shines through and partners beautifully with the basil and sweet jasmine rice.

Serves 4

5 to 10 minutes

10 minutes

1 tablespoon peanut oil
or vegetable oil
½ cup chopped onion,
any color
2 cloves garlic, minced
2 large eggs, lightly beaten
2 cups cooked jasmine rice,
or any cooked rice
2 tablespoons oyster sauce
2 tablespoons soy sauce
2 ½ to 3 cups cubed cooked
chicken from the Orange
Chicken (page 73), or
any cooked chicken
¼ cup chopped fresh basil
Salt and freshly ground
black pepper

1. Heat the peanut oil (or vegetable oil) in a large skillet or wok over medium-high heat. Add the onion, and cook for 3 to 5 minutes, until soft. Add the garlic, and cook for 30 seconds. Push the onion and garlic to the side of the pan, and add the eggs to the other side. Cook until the eggs are scrambled and still moist.

2. Add the rice, oyster sauce, and soy sauce, and stir to coat.

3. Fold in the chicken, and cook for 3 minutes to heat through. Fold in the fresh basil.

4. Season to taste with salt and black pepper, and serve.

BEEF AND PORK

Skirt Steak *with* Roasted Red Pepper Relish

This juicy steak is ultra-flavorful thanks to a vinaigrette-style marinade of balsamic vinegar, olive oil, dijon mustard, and garlic. Flavor seeps into every inch of the fork-tender meat. And the leftover steak from this meal works in all recipes in this book that call for cooked steak.

Serves 4, with leftover steak for a future meal

10 minutes

10 to 15 minutes

FOR THE STEAK:

3 tablespoons balsamic vinegar

1 tablespoon olive oil, plus
    more for brushing the pan

1 teaspoon dijon mustard

2 cloves garlic, minced

Salt and freshly ground
    black pepper

1 skirt steak, about 3
    pounds, or 2 smaller
    skirt steaks, about 1 ¼
    to 1 ½ pounds each

FOR THE ROASTED RED PEPPER RELISH:

1 cup chopped roasted
    red peppers, from
    water-packed jar

3 tablespoons chopped
    fresh parsley or basil

2 tablespoons minced
    red onion

Salt and freshly ground
    black pepper

1. In a large zip-top bag or container with a lid, combine the balsamic vinegar, olive oil, dijon mustard, garlic, ½ teaspoon salt, and ¼ teaspoon black pepper. Add the steak, and turn to coat. If you have the time, marinate for 30 minutes or up to 10 hours in the refrigerator.

2. Coat a large grill pan or griddle with olive oil, and preheat to medium-high. Remove the steak from the marinade, discard the marinade, and add the steak to the hot pan. Cook for 3 to 5 minutes per side for rare to medium-rare (140°F on an instant-read thermometer for rare), or longer for more fully cooked steak. Remove the steak from the heat, and let rest for 5 minutes.

3. Meanwhile, to make the relish, in a medium bowl, combine the roasted red peppers, fresh parsley (or basil), and red onion. Mix well, and season to taste with salt and black pepper.

4. Slice the steak crosswise, against the grain, into thin strips.

5. Reserve half of the steak for the Cheesy Steak and Potato Hash (page 82) or another future meal. Refrigerate for up to 3 days.

6. Serve the remaining steak with the roasted red pepper relish spooned over top.

SERVING SUGGESTION: For a complete and filling meal, serve the steak with your favorite raw or steamed vegetable and a starchy side, such as rice, beans, pasta, potatoes, sweet potatoes, quinoa, couscous, or whole grain bread. For more inspiration, check out my Meal Prep 101 tips 23, 24, and 25.

Round Two
Cheesy Steak *and* Potato Hash

Tender steak, golden brown potatoes, and a blanket of cheddar cheese—pretty much pure comfort in a skillet. And since all the seasoning is already embedded in the steak, there's very little prep work here. A quick seasoning of the potatoes, and you're ready to go.

Serves 4

5 to 10 minutes

20 to 25 minutes

3 tablespoons olive oil, divided

1 ½ pounds small red potatoes, cut into 1-inch pieces

1 teaspoon garlic powder

1 teaspoon onion powder

½ teaspoon paprika

Salt and freshly ground black pepper

2 cups diced cooked steak from the Skirt Steak with Roasted Red Pepper Relish (page 81), or any cooked steak

1 cup shredded cheddar cheese

Chopped green onions for serving

Ketchup for serving

1. Preheat the oven to 400°F. Coat a large, oven-safe skillet or shallow baking dish with 1 tablespoon of the olive oil.

2. In a large bowl, combine the remaining 2 tablespoons of olive oil, potatoes, garlic powder, onion powder, paprika, ½ teaspoon salt, and ¼ teaspoon black pepper, and toss to coat. Transfer the potatoes to the prepared pan, and bake for 15 minutes.

3. Fold the steak into the potatoes, top everything with the cheese, and return the pan to the oven for 10 to 15 minutes, until the potatoes are golden brown and the cheese melts.

4. Top with green onions, and serve with ketchup on the side.

GOOD TO KNOW
You can serve this dish for dinner, breakfast, or brunch! Nestle a few poached or fried eggs on top, and you'll have a feast for a crowd.

GOOD TO KNOW

Coating the steak with cornstarch before cooking helps seal in the steak's juices, thickens the sauce, and creates a crisp crust on the meat.

Round One
Thai Basil Beef

Tender steak strips, infused with a savory soy- and garlic-infused sauce, tossed with caramelized bell peppers and onion. Think of this dish when you're craving stir-fry with a twist. Why a twist? Because instead of using more traditional cilantro and/or green onions, we use Thai basil, which has a stronger flavor than its sweet basil cousin and delivers a licorice-like, anise flavor and peppery nuance. If you can't find Thai basil, regular basil also works and adds great complexity to the dish.

Serves 4, with leftover steak for a future meal

10 to 15 minutes

10 minutes

1 skirt steak, about 3 pounds, or 2 smaller skirt steaks, about 1 ¼ to 1 ½ pounds each, cut across the grain into thin strips

1 tablespoon cornstarch

2 tablespoons vegetable oil, divided

2 bell peppers, any color, seeded and thinly sliced

½ cup thinly sliced onion, any color

2 to 3 cloves garlic, minced

3 tablespoons soy sauce

2 teaspoons oyster sauce

1 teaspoon granulated sugar

½ cup Thai basil leaves, or regular basil leaves, plus more for serving

1. In a large bowl, combine the beef and cornstarch, and toss to coat the beef evenly.

2. Heat 1 tablespoon of the vegetable oil in a large skillet or wok over medium-high heat. Add the beef, and sear until just browned. Transfer the steak to a plate, and set aside.

3. Add the remaining tablespoon of vegetable oil to the pan with the bell peppers and onion. Cook for 3 to 5 minutes, until soft. Add the garlic, and cook for 30 seconds.

4. Return the steak to the pan with the soy sauce, oyster sauce, and sugar. Toss to combine.

5. Add the fresh basil, and cook until the leaves just wilt.

6. Reserve half of the steak (without the peppers and onion) for the Steak Street Tacos (page 86) or another future meal. Refrigerate for up to 3 days.

7. Top the remaining steak, peppers, and onion with fresh basil leaves, and serve.

SERVING SUGGESTION: Since this savory sauce is so sublime, I suggest you serve the meat and vegetables with rice (I prefer jasmine here), Asian noodles, or your favorite grain.

Steak Street Tacos

Handheld heaven! These delectable tacos feature smoky beef, sweet peppers, caramelized onions, and just enough fiery jalapeño to add a delightful amount of heat. Ready in minutes and served with a variety of fun toppings.

Serves 4

10 to 15 minutes

10 minutes

1 teaspoon liquid smoke

1 tablespoon Worcestershire sauce

2 ½ to 3 cups thinly sliced cooked steak from the Thai Basil Beef (page 85), or any cooked steak

Salt and freshly ground black pepper

1 tablespoon olive oil, or vegetable oil

1 cup sliced onion, any color

1 bell pepper, any color, seeded and sliced

1 jalapeño pepper, seeded and sliced

Street taco-size flour tortillas (about 2 to 3 per person), warmed if desired

FOR SERVING (ALL OPTIONAL, BUT AWESOME ADDITIONS):

Shredded lettuce

Shredded Mexican cheese blend or cheddar cheese

Crumbled cotija cheese

Fresh cilantro leaves

Chopped green onions

Mild, medium, or hot salsa

Hot sauce

1. In a medium bowl, combine the liquid smoke and Worcestershire sauce. Add the steak, and toss to coat.

2. Heat the olive oil (or vegetable oil) in a large skillet over medium-high heat. Add the onion, bell pepper, and jalapeño, and cook for 3 to 5 minutes, until soft. Season the vegetables with salt and black pepper.

3. Add the steak, and cook for 1 to 2 minutes to heat through.

4. Serve the steak and vegetables in the tortillas with optional toppings on the side.

GOOD TO KNOW

I prefer skirt steak for dishes like this because the steak has just enough marbling (fat) coursing through the meat to keep it moist and juicy. I think flank steak is a tougher cut (there's not as much marbling), but you can swap that in for the skirt if you want. Truth is, any steak cut will work here, so choose your favorite.

Round One
Beef Patty Melts

This recipe may have a short ingredient list, but flavors soar! The beef patties are simply seasoned with salt, pepper, and Worcestershire sauce, but Worcestershire sauce adds a tremendous amount of flavor and tenderizes the meat at the same time. Then, the patties are topped with caramelized onions and melty swiss cheese and nestled between slices of tangy rye bread.

Serves 4, with leftover beef patties for a future meal

10 minutes

20 minutes

8 tablespoons unsalted butter

1 ½ cups sliced onion, any color

2 pounds lean ground beef

1 tablespoon Worcestershire sauce

Salt and freshly ground black pepper

8 slices swiss cheese

8 slices rye bread, or bread of choice

1. Melt 2 tablespoons of the butter in a large skillet over medium-low heat. Add the onions, and cook until brown and caramelized, about 15 minutes, stirring frequently.

2. Meanwhile, in a medium bowl, combine the ground beef, Worcestershire sauce, 1 teaspoon salt, and ½ teaspoon black pepper. Mix well, and shape the mixture into 8 equal patties.

3. Melt 2 tablespoons of the butter in a separate skillet over medium heat. When the butter is bubbling, add the patties, and cook until you reach your desired level of doneness (about 5 to 7 minutes for medium).

4. Set aside 4 patties for the Beefy Lasagna Bowls (page 90) or another future meal. Refrigerate for up to 3 days.

5. To assemble the patty melts, arrange 4 slices of bread on a flat surface. Top the bread with a slice of cheese, hamburger patty, caramelized onions, another slice of cheese, and another slice of bread.

6. Melt 2 tablespoons of the butter in a clean skillet over medium heat. Add the patty melts, and cook until the bottom is golden brown. Transfer the patty melts to a plate so you can add the remaining butter to the skillet. When the butter is bubbling, return the patty melts to the pan to cook the second side. Cook until the bottom is golden brown and crisp and the cheese melts.

Round Two
Beefy Lasagna Bowls

Hearty lasagna noodles, cooked in a zesty sauce of tomatoes, onion, garlic, oregano, and basil and served in bowls like stew. And since the noodles cook directly in the sauce—not a pot of water—they're incredibly flavorful, from the first tender bite to the last.

Serves 4

10 minutes

20 minutes

1 tablespoon olive oil

½ cup chopped onion, any color

2 cloves garlic, minced

1 teaspoon dried basil

1 teaspoon dried oregano

Salt and freshly ground
    black pepper

4 cups tomato sauce

3 to 4 cups beef broth, or
    chicken broth, or water

8 ounces lasagna noodles,
    broken into 2-inch
    pieces (about 8 to
    9 full noodles)

4 cubed cooked beef patties
    from the Beef Patty
    Melts (page 89), or ¾
    pound ground beef,
    browned and drained

½ cup shredded mozzarella
    cheese, plus more
    for serving

2 tablespoons grated
    parmesan cheese, plus
    more for serving

Chopped fresh parsley or
    basil for serving

1. Heat the olive oil in a large stock pot or saucepan over medium-high heat. Add the onion, and cook for 3 to 5 minutes, until soft. Add the garlic, basil, oregano, ½ teaspoon salt, and ¼ teaspoon black pepper, and stir to coat. Cook for 30 seconds, until the herbs are fragrant.

2. Add the tomato sauce and broth, and bring to a low boil. Add the noodles, and cook for 10 to 12 minutes, reducing the temperature as necessary to keep the liquid at a low boil (as the liquid reduces, the sauce gets more vigorous), stirring frequently. Reduce the heat to low, fold in the beef, mozzarella, and parmesan cheese, and simmer for 2 more minutes to heat through and melt the cheese.

3. Ladle the mixture into bowls, and top with a little more mozzarella and fresh parsley or basil. Serve with extra parmesan cheese on the side.

GOOD TO KNOW
For the sauce, we use tomato sauce kicked up with onion, garlic, oregano, and basil. If you prefer, you can use 4 cups of your favorite store-bought marinara sauce instead. When using store-bought marinara sauce, if desired, you can leave out the oregano, basil, salt, and pepper. Since different brands vary, check the dish for seasoning (salt and pepper) just before serving.

GOOD TO KNOW

If you make extra tzatziki, you can use it as the dressing for the Greek Rice Bowls (page 229).

Round One

Mediterranean Meatballs *with* Tzatziki

These marvelous meatballs are scented with cumin and studded with onion, garlic, parsley, and mint. They're insanely moist and savory, and they partner perfectly with the cooling essence of tzatziki—a creamy, lemony, cucumber- and dill-spiked yogurt dip.

Serves 4, with leftover meatballs for a future meal

10 minutes

20 minutes

FOR THE MEATBALLS:

2 pounds lean ground beef

½ cup diced red onion

3 to 4 cloves garlic, minced

2 tablespoons chopped fresh mint

2 tablespoons chopped fresh parsley

1 teaspoon ground cumin

1 teaspoon dried oregano

Salt and freshly ground black pepper

FOR THE TZATZIKI:

1 cup plain Greek yogurt

½ cup diced English/ seedless cucumber, peeled or unpeeled

3 tablespoons chopped fresh dill

2 cloves garlic, minced or grated

Juice of one lemon

1. Preheat the oven to 400°F. Line a large baking sheet with parchment paper or aluminum foil.

2. To make the meatballs, in a large bowl, combine the beef, onion, garlic, mint, fresh parsley, cumin, oregano, 1 teaspoon salt, and ½ teaspoon black pepper. Mix well, and shape the mixture into 32 to 36 meatballs.

3. Transfer the meatballs to the prepared pan, and roast for 20 to 25 minutes, until browned and cooked through.

4. Meanwhile, to make the tzatziki, combine all ingredients in a medium bowl, and mix well. Season to taste with salt and black pepper.

5. Reserve half of the meatballs for the Moroccan Meatball Soup (page 94) or another future meal. Refrigerate for up to 3 days.

6. Serve the remaining meatballs with the tzatziki on the side.

PREP AHEAD TIP: The meatballs can be assembled and refrigerated for up to 24 hours before baking. The tzatziki can be prepared up to 24 hours in advance. Refrigerate until ready to serve.

Round Two
Moroccan Meatball Soup

The ultimate bowl of comfort. This hearty soup boasts savory meatballs (either from the Mediterranean Meatballs with Tzatziki, page 93, or any cooked meatballs of choice), aromatic vegetables, fresh spinach, and little pearls of tender couscous. The broth is scented with cinnamon, and the soup is served with a generous amount of fresh cilantro and green onions.

Serves 4

10 to 15 minutes

15 minutes

1 tablespoon olive oil

1 cup chopped carrots

1 cup chopped celery

1 teaspoon ground cumin

Pinch of cinnamon

4 cups beef broth

1 cup pearled couscous

16 to 18 cooked meatballs
    from the Mediterranean
    Meatballs with Tzatziki
    (page 93), or any cooked
    meatballs, quartered

Salt and freshly ground
    black pepper

4 cups baby spinach leaves

¼ cup fresh cilantro leaves

2 tablespoons chopped
    green onions

1. Heat the olive oil in a large stock pot or saucepan over medium-high heat. Add the carrots and celery, and cook for 3 to 5 minutes, until soft. Add the cumin and cinnamon, and toss to coat. Cook for 30 seconds, until the spices are fragrant.

2. Add the broth, and bring to a low boil. Add the couscous, and cook for 3 minutes. Add the meatballs and spinach, and cook for 3 to 4 more minutes, until the couscous is tender.

3. Remove the pan from the heat, and fold in the fresh cilantro and green onions. Season to taste with salt and black pepper, and serve.

GOOD TO KNOW

I used pearled couscous here because I like the bigger balls of pasta for soup recipes. If desired, you can use regular couscous or your favorite pasta shape. Since it's a soup recipe, smaller pasta shapes (such as orzo and acini de pepe) are preferred. For a gluten-free soup, you can also use rice.

Round One
Steak au Poivre

Restaurant-quality steak in the comfort of your own home! Although this ingredient list is short, each element plays an important role in the dish. The peppercorns are nutty and fresh, the shallots are sweet and garlicky, the cognac adds a fruity/caramel quality, and the cream ties everything together, creating a buttery mouthfeel.

Serves 4, with leftover steak for a future meal

10 minutes

20 minutes

FOR THE STEAK:

6 boneless beef top-loin (strip)
    or round steaks, about
    6 to 8 ounces each
3 tablespoons whole black
    peppercorns
1 ½ tablespoons salt
1 tablespoon vegetable oil

FOR THE SAUCE:

4 tablespoons unsalted
    butter, divided
⅓ cup finely chopped
    shallots, or red onion
½ cup cognac, or other brandy
½ cup heavy cream
Chopped fresh parsley for
    serving, optional

1. Preheat the oven to 200°F.
2. Place the peppercorns in a freezer bag, and pound them with a meat mallet or the bottom of a heavy skillet until coarsely crushed.
3. Pat the steaks dry, and press the crushed black pepper and salt into both sides.
4. Heat the vegetable oil in a large skillet over medium-high heat. Working in batches to prevent crowding the pan, add the steaks, and cook for 3 to 5 minutes per side for rare to medium-rare (140°F on an instant-read thermometer for rare), or longer for more fully cooked steak.
5. Transfer the steaks to a plate, and tent with aluminum foil while you make the sauce.
6. Discard any fat from the skillet, and return the pan to medium-low heat. Add 2 tablespoons of the butter and shallots (or red onion), and cook for 3 to 5 minutes, until golden brown, scraping up any browned bits from the bottom of the pan and incorporating them into the sauce.
7. Remove the pan from the heat, add the cognac or brandy (this prevents the alcohol from igniting), and return the pan to the heat. Simmer for 2 to 3 minutes, until the sauce reduces by half. Add the heavy cream and any meat juices that have accumulated on the plate. Simmer for 3 minutes, until the sauce reduces by half again.

8. Add the remaining 2 tablespoons of butter, and cook over low heat, swirling the skillet, until the butter is incorporated.

9. Reserve 2 steaks for the Easy Steak Gyros with Yogurt-Mint Sauce (page 100) or another future meal. Refrigerate for up to 3 days.

10. Spoon the sauce over the remaining steaks. Top with fresh parsley (if using), and serve.

SERVING SUGGESTION: For a complete and filling meal, serve the steak with your favorite raw or steamed vegetable and a starchy side, such as rice, beans, pasta, potatoes, sweet potatoes, quinoa, couscous, or whole grain bread. For more inspiration, check out my Meal Prep 101 tips 23, 24, and 25.

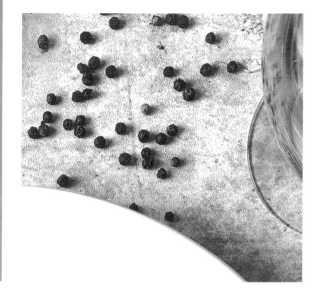

Easy Steak Gyros *with* Yogurt-Mint Sauce

Strips of juicy beef seasoned with Greek herbs and piled onto warm flat-bread or pocketless pitas. What really makes these handheld treats shine is the toppings—a tangy yogurt-mint sauce (that's sweetened *and* tinted with paprika), crisp cucumber, red onion, fresh tomatoes, and salty feta cheese.

Serves 4

10 to 15 minutes

5 minutes

FOR THE YOGURT-MINT SAUCE:

½ cup plain Greek yogurt

2 teaspoons chopped fresh mint

½ teaspoon dried oregano

½ teaspoon paprika

Salt and freshly ground
    black pepper

FOR THE STEAK GYROS:

2 tablespoons vegetable oil

1 teaspoon Greek seasoning,
    or Italian seasoning

2 to 2 ½ cups thinly sliced
    steak from the Steak
    au Poivre (page 97),
    or any cooked steak

4 flatbreads or pocketless
    pitas, warmed if desired

1 cup sliced English/
    seedless cucumber,
    peeled or unpeeled

1 cup sliced red onion

½ cup cherry or grape
    tomatoes, sliced

Crumbled feta cheese

1. To make the yogurt-mint sauce, in a medium bowl, combine the yogurt, mint, oregano, and paprika. Mix well, and season to taste with salt and black pepper. Set aside.

2. Heat the vegetable oil in a large skillet over medium-low heat. Add the Greek seasoning (or Italian seasoning), and cook for 1 minute, until the herbs are fragrant. Add the steak, and cook for 1 to 2 minutes, until hot.

3. Spread some of the yogurt mixture on the flatbreads (or pocketless pitas). Top with the steak, cucumber, red onion, tomatoes, and feta. Serve with extra yogurt sauce on the side.

GOOD TO KNOW

This recipe calls for Greek seasoning, a spice blend consisting of Mediterranean herbs (oregano, basil, parsley, dill, and sometimes rosemary). If you don't have Greek seasoning, you may substitute Italian seasoning as it has a similar blend of basil, parsley, oregano, rosemary, and thyme.

Round One
Pasta *with* Easy Bolognese

Savory ground beef, aromatic herbs, and sweet/tangy tomatoes— transformed into a sauce and ladled over pasta. Every spoonful delivers nuances of sweet, savory, salty, floral, and nutty. I'm pretty sure this is the only meat sauce recipe you will ever need.

Serves 4, with leftover Bolognese sauce for a future meal

10 minutes

15 to 20 minutes

1 pound penne, or pasta of choice

1 tablespoon olive oil

½ cup chopped onion, any color

2 cloves garlic, minced

2 pounds lean ground beef

1 tablespoon Italian seasoning

Salt and freshly ground black pepper

3 cups tomato sauce

Shredded parmesan cheese for serving

Chopped fresh basil or parsley for serving

1. Cook the pasta according to the package directions. Drain, and cover with aluminum foil to keep warm.

2. Meanwhile, heat the olive oil in a large stock pot or saucepan over medium-high heat. Add the onion, and cook for 3 to 5 minutes, until soft. Add the garlic, and cook for 30 seconds.

3. Add the beef, and cook until browned, breaking up the meat as it cooks. Add the Italian seasoning, ½ teaspoon salt, and ¼ teaspoon black pepper, and stir to coat. Cook for 1 minute, until the herbs are fragrant.

4. Add the tomato sauce, and bring to a simmer. Reduce the heat to medium-low, and simmer for 10 minutes.

5. Reserve half of the sauce for the Greek Stuffed Peppers (page 104) or another future meal. Refrigerate for up to 3 days.

6. Transfer the pasta to individual plates or shallow bowls, and top with the Bolognese sauce. Top with parmesan cheese and fresh basil or parsley, and serve.

PREP AHEAD TIP: This is a great sauce to make in advance because it stores quite well when refrigerated and frozen. To make the sauce in advance, prepare it as directed, and then let it cool. Transfer the sauce to an airtight container, and refrigerate for up to 3 days or freeze for up to 3 months. Thaw overnight in the refrigerator. I suggest you double the recipe below and keep a batch in the freezer at all times!

Round Two

Greek Stuffed Peppers

Stuffed peppers transformed! These caramelized bell peppers are stuffed with a savory blend of seasoned beef (already seasoned from the Bolognese sauce on page 103) and oregano- and paprika-scented rice. You need little else for the filling since the meat sauce is already ultra-flavorful. Adding fresh parsley enlivens the dish and gives the meat sauce new life. The feta cheese on top finishes the dish and adds a wonderful salty/tangy quality.

Serves 4

5 minutes

25 minutes

2 cups cooked white rice

1 tablespoon unsalted butter

1 teaspoon dried oregano

1 teaspoon paprika

Salt and freshly ground
    black pepper

2 cups Bolognese sauce
    from the Pasta with
    Easy Bolognese
    (page 103), or 1
    pound ground beef,
    browned and drained

2 tablespoons chopped
    fresh parsley

4 to 6 bell peppers, any
    color, tops removed
    and reserved, seeds and
    membranes removed

½ cup crumbled feta cheese

1. Preheat the oven to 350°F.

2. Combine the rice, butter, oregano, paprika, ½ teaspoon salt, and ¼ teaspoon black pepper in a large bowl. Fold in the Bolognese sauce and fresh parsley.

3. Use a small spoon to fill the peppers with the mixture. Transfer the stuffed peppers to a shallow baking dish, and add about 1 cup of water to the bottom of the pan. Arrange the pepper tops alongside the peppers.

4. Cover loosely with aluminum foil, and bake for 20 minutes.

5. Uncover, top the peppers with the feta cheese, and bake for 5 more minutes, until the peppers are tender and the feta is golden.

You can use any variety of herbs you want in the butter. I used garlic, parsley, chives, and a little cilantro. I basically cleaned out my produce drawer. Use your favorite herbs—either one herb or a combination of many. The butter is so tasty, you'll always want it in your fridge to use on other dishes, such as pasta, rice, vegetables, baked potatoes, steak, chicken, pork, and bread. Don't worry. This recipe makes plenty of butter for leftovers. I used my remaining butter in mashed potatoes, and it was phenomenal.

Garlic and Herb Butter Burgers

One bite and you'll be smitten. Inside these juicy burgers lies a pat of garlic-and-herb-infused butter. Not only does butter keep the burgers beyond juicy, but as it melts, the garlic and herbs permeate every inch of the meat.

Serves 4, with leftover burgers for a future meal

15 minutes

15 minutes

FOR THE BUTTER:

⅓ cup unsalted butter, softened

3 tablespoons mixed fresh herbs of choice, such as parsley, basil, oregano, cilantro, and/or chives

2 cloves garlic, minced

Salt and freshly ground black pepper

FOR THE BURGERS:

2 ½ pounds lean ground beef

8 slices cheddar or American cheese, or cheese of choice

4 hamburger buns

Condiments and toppings of choice

1. In a small bowl, combine the butter, herbs, garlic, ¼ teaspoon salt, and a pinch of black pepper. Mix with the back of a spoon until blended.

2. Mound the butter mixture onto the center of a 12-inch piece of plastic wrap. Lift up the sides of the plastic, and use the wrap to shape the butter into a cylinder. Twist the ends to compress the butter into a cylinder.

3. Chill or freeze until firm (butter will keep for up to 5 days in the refrigerator and up to 3 months in the freezer).

4. To make the burgers, shape the beef into 8 patties. Press your thumb into the center of each patty, almost through to the other side but not quite, making a deep indentation.

5. Cut the chilled butter crosswise into ¼-inch-thick rounds. Place one butter round in the center of each burger, and form the meat around the butter, fully encasing the butter while reshaping the beef into a patty.

6. Coat a grill pan, skillet, or outdoor grill with cooking spray, and preheat to medium-high.

7. Add the burgers to the hot pan/grill, and cook until your desired level of doneness (about 5 to 7 minutes for medium).

8. Transfer the burgers to a plate and top with the cheese. Tent with aluminum foil. Let stand for 3 to 5 minutes; this allows flavors to sink into the meat.

9. Reserve 4 burgers for the Cheeseburger Noodles with Spinach (page 108) or another future meal. Refrigerate for up to 3 days.

10. Serve the remaining burgers on the buns with desired condiments.

Round Two

Cheeseburger Noodles *with* Spinach

Savory cheeseburger chunks and pasta tossed in an herby tomato sauce and smothered in cheese. Everything is cooked in one skillet (including the noodles), and this mind-blowing meal is ready in about 25 minutes.

Serves 4

10 minutes

15 minutes

3 cups tomato sauce

2 ½ cups beef broth

1 teaspoon dried parsley

4 cups egg noodles or yolk-free egg noodles (about 6 ounces)

4 cubed cooked cheeseburgers from the Garlic and Herb Butter Burgers (page 107), or any cooked burgers

3 cups baby spinach leaves

1 cup shredded cheddar cheese, or Mexican cheese blend, or a blend of cheddar and mozzarella cheeses

Salt and freshly ground black pepper

1. In a large stock pot or saucepan, whisk together the tomato sauce, broth, and dried parsley. Set the pan over medium-high heat, and bring to a low boil.

2. Add the egg noodles, partially cover, and cook for 10 minutes, until the noodles are tender, stirring frequently and reducing the temperature as necessary to keep the sauce at a low boil.

3. Fold in the cheeseburger pieces and spinach, and cook for 2 to 3 minutes to heat through and wilt the spinach. Fold in the cheese. Season to taste with salt and black pepper, and serve.

> **GOOD TO KNOW**
>
> I made this dish with yolk-free egg noodles because they're lighter than traditional egg noodles (which kept the dish from being overly heavy). As the pasta simmered in the sauce, the noodles softened and wove in and out of the beef mixture like scrumptious little waves. That said, you can use any pasta variety and/or shape you want.

Round One

Minute Steaks
with Chipotle Gravy

Buttery, fork-tender steaks simply seasoned with salt and pepper, pan-seared until golden and crisp, and then smothered in a smoky, satiny, easy gravy. This showstopping meal will change your opinion about "busy weeknight cooking" because you only need five ingredients and about 20 minutes to create a meal that appears to have taken hours.

Serves 4, with leftover steaks for a future meal

10 minutes

10 minutes

8 minute steaks or cube steaks, about 4 to 5 ounces each

Salt and freshly ground black pepper

¾ cup all-purpose flour

2 tablespoons vegetable oil

2 tablespoons unsalted butter

1 ½ cups half-and-half

1 tablespoon minced chipotle chiles in adobo sauce, or more/less to taste

Chopped fresh chives for serving

1. Season both sides of the steaks with salt and black pepper. Place the flour in a shallow dish, add the steaks, and turn to coat (reserve 1 tablespoon of the dredging flour for the gravy).

2. Heat the vegetable oil in a large skillet over medium heat. Working in batches to prevent crowding the pan, shake the excess flour from the steaks, and add them to the hot oil. Cook until browned and crisp on both sides, about 2 to 4 minutes per side. Transfer the steaks to a plate.

3. Melt the butter in the same skillet over medium heat. When the butter is bubbling, whisk in the remaining tablespoon of flour (used to dredge the steaks). Whisk in the half-and-half and chipotle chiles. Simmer until the sauce thickens to a gravy consistency, whisking frequently. Season to taste with salt and black pepper.

4. Reserve 4 of the steaks for the Steak Caesar Wraps (page 112) or another future meal. Refrigerate for up 3 days.

5. Pour the gravy over the remaining steaks, top with the fresh chives, and serve.

SERVING SUGGESTION: For a complete and filling meal, serve the steak with your favorite raw or steamed vegetable and a starchy side, such as rice, beans, pasta, potatoes, sweet potatoes, quinoa, couscous, or whole grain bread. For more inspiration, check out my Meal Prep 101 tips 23, 24, and 25.

Round Two

Steak Caesar Wraps

Skip takeout and, in just minutes, you can enjoy an unbelievable Caesar wrap sandwich made with just six ingredients. Each soft wrap is loaded with tender beef, crisp lettuce, crunchy croutons, nutty parmesan cheese, and creamy, store-bought Caesar dressing. The croutons not only add texture, but they also assert an herby-salty flavor that perfectly complements the steak.

Serves 4

10 to 15 minutes

4 cups chopped romaine lettuce

3 tablespoons Caesar dressing

¼ cup crumbled or crushed croutons (coarse crumbs)

4 large tortilla wraps or flatbreads of choice

3–4 cups thinly sliced cooked steak from the Minute Steaks with Chipotle Gravy (page 111), or any cooked steak

Shredded parmesan cheese for serving

1. In a large bowl, combine the lettuce and Caesar dressing. Toss to coat. Fold in the croutons.
2. Arrange the wraps on a flat surface, and top with the lettuce and steak. Sprinkle a little parmesan cheese over top.
3. Roll up tightly, and serve.

Round One

Sesame Beef *with* Broccoli

This beef is shimmering in a soy-, sesame-, and garlic-infused sauce and then piled onto fluffy rice with tender-crisp, vibrant broccoli. This quick-and-easy, savory meal is ready in less than 25 minutes, gluten free, and undeniably healthy.

Serves 4, with leftover beef for a future meal

10 to 15 minutes

10 minutes

⅔ cup beef broth, or water

⅓ cup soy sauce

2 tablespoons cornstarch

1 ½ teaspoons sesame oil

½ teaspoon garlic powder

½ teaspoon onion powder

2 pounds lean ground beef

Salt and freshly ground
   black pepper

2 cups broccoli florets,
   blanched or steamed until
   crisp-tender if desired

2 cups cooked rice of choice
   (I use jasmine)

2 tablespoons toasted sesame
   seeds* for serving

Chopped green onions
   for serving

1. In a small bowl, whisk together the broth (or water), soy sauce, cornstarch, sesame oil, garlic powder, and onion powder. Set aside.

2. Brown the beef in a large skillet over medium-high heat, breaking up the meat as it cooks. Add the soy sauce mixture, and bring to a simmer. Simmer for 2 to 3 minutes, until the sauce thickens. Season to taste with salt and black pepper. Reserve 1 cup of the beef for the Beef and Bean Empanadas (page 116) or another future meal. Refrigerate for up to 3 days.

3. Add the broccoli to the remaining beef, and cook for 1 to 2 minutes to heat through.

4. Spoon the beef mixture over the rice, and top with sesame seeds and green onions.

---

* You can find toasted sesame seeds next to the regular sesame seeds in the spice aisle. If you'd rather toast them yourself, add the raw seeds to a dry skillet, and set the pan over medium heat. Cook until golden brown, about 2 to 3 minutes, shaking the pan frequently to promote even cooking and to prevent scorching.

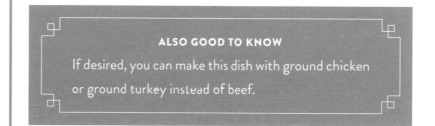

ALSO GOOD TO KNOW
If desired, you can make this dish with ground chicken or ground turkey instead of beef.

Beef *and* Bean Empanadas

Inside each pocket of buttery, flaky pie crust lies a perfectly seasoned blend of juicy ground beef, savory black beans, green chiles, warming spices, and gooey Mexican cheese. The pastry is crisp and golden, and the filling is moist and cheesy. Quite possibly the world's most perfect bite.

Serves 4 to 6

15 minutes

15 minutes

1 cup cooked ground beef from the Sesame Beef with Broccoli (page 115), or ½ pound ground beef, browned and drained

½ cup canned seasoned black beans or chili beans of choice, or any canned beans, rinsed and drained (don't rinse the seasoned beans)

1 (4-ounce) can diced green chiles

2 tablespoons tomato paste

1 teaspoon chili powder

1 teaspoon ground cumin

Salt and freshly ground black pepper

½ cup shredded Mexican cheese blend

2 (9-inch) refrigerated pie crusts

1 egg, lightly beaten

Salsa of choice for serving

1. Preheat the oven to 400°F. Line a large baking sheet with parchment paper or aluminum foil.

2. In a large skillet, combine the beef, beans, green chiles, tomato paste, chili powder, and cumin. Set the pan over medium heat, and bring to a simmer. Fold in the cheese, season to taste with salt and pepper, and stir until the cheese melts. Remove the pan from the heat.

3. Unroll the pie crusts onto a clean, flat surface. Using a 4-inch round pastry cutter, cut circles from the dough (combine the scraps, roll them out, and cut again until all the dough is used). You should have 12 (4-inch) rounds.

4. Spoon about 2 tablespoons of the beef mixture into the center of each circle. Fold the dough over, and use a fork to seal the curved edge.

5. Transfer the empanadas to the prepared pan in a single layer, not touching each other. Brush with the egg.

6. Bake for 15 minutes, until golden brown. (It's OK if some burst open; it makes for a rustic presentation!)

7. Cool slightly before serving with the salsa.

GOOD TO KNOW

No pastry cutter? No problem! To make 4-inch circles, you can use any small bowl you have or the top of a glass or mug. I used a small prep bowl.

ALSO GOOD TO KNOW

In this recipe, lots of flavor comes from the beans and chiles. I called for seasoned beans, meaning canned beans packed in a savory sauce. You can choose any seasoned beans you like, including chili beans. If you have regular beans and don't want to run to the store, no problem, you can use them instead; just rinse regular beans before using to remove excess salt.

GOOD TO KNOW

The peanut dipping sauce can be served room temperature or warm and can be made as thin or as thick as you like.

Steak Skewers *with* Peanut Dip

This colorful and healthy meal features seared strips of steak, bell peppers, and onion served with a savory/nutty peanut dipping sauce. And since we start with store-bought black bean sauce, the skewers come together in a flash. The peanut dip is equally easy, as it's made with pantry staples and completely customizable in terms of heat level.

Serves 4, with leftover steak for a future meal

15 minutes

10 minutes

FOR THE SKEWERS:

2 pounds flank or skirt steak, cut against the grain into long thin strips

2 bell peppers, any color, seeded and cut into 1-inch pieces

1 red onion, cut into 1-inch pieces

Black bean sauce of choice

Salt and freshly ground black pepper

FOR THE PEANUT DIP:

5 tablespoons smooth peanut butter

2 tablespoons soy sauce

2 teaspoons hot sauce of choice, or more/less to taste

½ teaspoon sesame oil

1 to 2 tablespoons water, as needed

Fresh cilantro leaves for serving

1. Skewer alternating pieces of steak, bell pepper, and red onion on metal or wooden skewers (soak wooden skewers in water before using so they don't burn). Drizzle the skewers with the black bean sauce, and season with salt and black pepper.

2. Coat an outdoor grill, grill pan, or griddle with olive or vegetable oil, and preheat to medium-high.

3. Add the skewers, and cook for 4 to 6 minutes for rare to medium-rare (140°F on an instant-read thermometer for rare) or longer for more fully cooked meat, turning the skewers occasionally during cooking.

4. Transfer the skewers to a plate, cover with aluminum foil, and let rest for 5 minutes.

5. Meanwhile, to make the peanut sauce, combine all the ingredients but the cilantro, adding water as necessary to reach your desired consistency. If desired, microwave the sauce for 1 minute to warm.

6. Reserve half of the skewers for the Honey Garlic Steak (page 120) or another future meal. Refrigerate for up to 3 days.

7. Serve the remaining skewers with the fresh cilantro and peanut sauce.

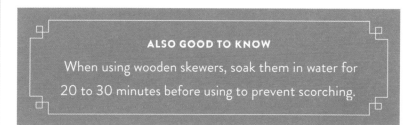

ALSO GOOD TO KNOW
When using wooden skewers, soak them in water for 20 to 30 minutes before using to prevent scorching.

Round Two
Honey Garlic Steak

These juicy nuggets of beef are ultra-moist and laced with sweet honey, salty soy, and zingy garlic. It's an explosion of flavor, from the sticky outside to the tender middle.

🍴	Serves 4
🥄	5 to 10 minutes
🔥	5 minutes

⅓ cup soy sauce

3 tablespoons honey

2 tablespoons water

2 to 3 cloves garlic, minced

3 cups cubed cooked
    steak from the Steak
    Skewers with Peanut
    Dip (page 119), or
    any cooked steak

1 tablespoon unsalted butter

Salt and freshly ground
    black pepper

Chopped green onions
    for serving

1. In a large skillet, combine the soy sauce, honey, water, and garlic. Set the pan over medium-high heat, and bring to a simmer. Add the steak and butter, and cook for 2 to 3 minutes, until the steak is warmed through, the butter melts, and the sauce thickens. Season to taste with salt and black pepper.

2. Top with green onions, and serve.

GOOD TO KNOW
You can choose your favorite cut of steak for this dish. Pretty much any steak works here (except stew meat). That means you can use thin strips of flank or skirt steak or chunks of lean steak like round and sirloin.

PREP AHEAD TIP: The soy sauce mixture can be prepared up to 24 hours in advance. To save time on meal-prep day, cut the steak up to 24 hours in advance and refrigerate until ready to cook.

SERVING SUGGESTION: Serve the beef and sauce in lettuce leaves, over rice, or over your favorite grain.

Cube Steaks *with* Easy Gravy

This ingredient list might be short, but the flavor in this dish is huge. The tender cube steaks need just a few minutes in the pan before they're smothered in a quick-and-easy, onion-rich gravy. The onions are sweet and caramelized, and the sauce is scented with sweet paprika and tangy Worcestershire sauce. This gravy is one that you'll be making repeatedly, especially because it's equally delicious over chicken and pork.

Serves 4, with leftover steaks for a future meal

5 to 10 minutes

15 to 20 minutes

8 cube steaks, about 4 to 5 ounces each

1 teaspoon paprika

Salt and freshly ground black pepper

4 tablespoons unsalted butter, divided

1 cup sliced yellow or red onion

2 tablespoons all-purpose flour

1 ½ cups beef broth

1 teaspoon Worcestershire sauce

Chopped fresh parsley for serving

1. Season both sides of the steaks with the paprika, salt, and pepper. Set aside.

2. Melt 2 tablespoons of the butter in a large skillet over medium heat. Add the onion, and cook for 3 to 5 minutes, until soft. Transfer the onions to a plate, and increase the temperature to medium-high.

3. Working in batches to prevent crowding the pan, add the steaks, and cook for 3 to 5 minutes per side for rare to medium-rare (140°F on an instant-read thermometer for rare) or longer for more fully cooked steak.

4. Transfer 4 of the steaks to the plate with the onions. Reserve the remaining steaks for the Easy One-Pot Beef Goulash (page 124) or another future meal. Refrigerate for up to 3 days.

5. Melt the remaining 2 tablespoons of butter in the same skillet over medium-high heat, scraping up any browned bits from the bottom of the pan and incorporating them into the butter. Whisk in the flour until blended. Whisk in the broth and Worcestershire sauce, and bring to a simmer. Reduce the heat to medium-low, and simmer for 2 to 3 minutes, until the sauce thickens.

6. Return the reserved steaks and onions to the pan with any accumulated juices from the plate. Simmer for 1 minute to heat through. Top with fresh parsley, and serve.

Easy One-Pot Beef Goulash

Truth be told, goulash is typically made with ground beef, but cube steak mimics ground beef perfectly and adds great texture to this easy, one-pot stew. In every spoonful, you can enjoy seasoned beef, herb-scented vegetables, tender macaroni, and plenty of cheddar cheese.

Serves 4

10 minutes

20 minutes

1 tablespoon olive oil

1 cup chopped onion, any color

1 bell pepper, any color, seeded and chopped

2 cloves garlic, minced

1 teaspoon paprika

Salt and freshly ground black pepper

2 (28-ounce) cans crushed tomatoes

2 cups chicken broth, or beef broth

2 teaspoons Worcestershire sauce

2 cups elbow macaroni

1 ½ to 2 cups cubed cooked steak from the Cube Steaks with Easy Gravy (page 123), or any cooked steaks, or ½ pound ground beef, browned and drained

1 cup shredded cheddar cheese

Chopped fresh parsley for serving

1. Heat the olive oil in a large stock pot or saucepan over medium-high heat. Add the onion and bell pepper, and cook for 3 to 5 minutes, until soft. Add the garlic, and cook for 30 seconds. Add the paprika, ½ teaspoon salt, and ¼ teaspoon black pepper, and stir to coat.

2. Add the crushed tomatoes, broth, and Worcestershire sauce, and bring to a low boil.

3. Add the macaroni, and return to a low boil. Partially cover, and simmer for 10 minutes, until the pasta is tender, stirring frequently.

4. Add the steak, and cook for 2 to 3 minutes to heat through. Stir in the cheese.

5. Ladle the mixture into bowls, and top with fresh parsley.

GOOD TO KNOW

If you don't have leftover cube steak, you may substitute 1 pound lean ground beef, cooked.

SERVING SUGGESTION: Since goulash features meat, vegetables, and pasta, it's a complete and wholesome meal. If desired, serve a fresh green salad on the side and call it a day!

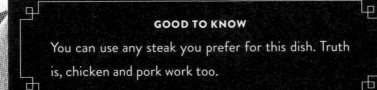

GOOD TO KNOW

You can use any steak you prefer for this dish. Truth is, chicken and pork work too.

ALSO GOOD TO KNOW

Don't rush the onions! For the best result and perfectly cooked onions, let them brown slowly over medium-low heat. You want the onions sweet and caramelized, not seared and blackened.

Round One
French Onion Steaks

All the flavors of the classic soup with the addition of juicy steak! This unique meal showcases wine-infused caramelized onions, chewy-crisp toasted bread, stretchy swiss cheese, and perfectly cooked steaks. Totally unique and likely to become a staple in your home.

Serves 4, with leftover steaks for a future meal

10 minutes

20 minutes

2 tablespoons unsalted butter

1 ½ cups thinly sliced yellow onion

8 lean steaks of choice, about 2 ½ pounds total

Salt and freshly ground black pepper

½ cup white wine, sherry, or marsala

½ cup beef broth

4 slices french bread/ baguette, cut crosswise into ½-inch-thick slices, toasted

4 slices swiss cheese, about 4 ounces

Chopped fresh parsley for serving, optional

1. Melt the butter in a large skillet over medium-low heat. Add the onions and cook until brown and caramelized, about 15 minutes, stirring frequently.

2. Meanwhile, season the steaks with salt and black pepper. Coat a large skillet, griddle, or grill pan with olive oil, and preheat to medium-high. Add the steaks, and cook for 3 to 5 minutes per side for rare to medium-rare (140°F on an instant-read thermometer for rare) or longer for more fully cooked meat. Remove the steaks from the heat, transfer half of them to an oven-safe baking dish or skillet, and tent with aluminum foil while you finish the onions.

3. Reserve the remaining steaks for the Easy Mongolian Beef Bowls (page 128) or another future meal. Refrigerate for up to 3 days.

4. When the onions are deep brown, add the wine, and bring to a simmer. Simmer until the liquid reduces by half. Add the broth, and simmer until the liquid reduces by half again. Season to taste with salt and pepper.

5. Preheat the broiler.

6. Spoon some of the onions over the steaks, and arrange the rest of the onions and liquid alongside the steaks. Top the steaks with the bread slices and cheese. Place the pan under the broiler (about 4 to 5 inches from the heat source), and cook until the cheese melts, about 1 to 2 minutes.

7. Top with fresh parsley (if using), and serve.

Round Two

Easy Mongolian Beef Bowls

Ginger and garlic are the star flavors in this dish, and they make the base of a glossy, sweet, and salty glaze. And while the steaks from the French Onion Steaks (page 127) work well here, you can use any cooked steak instead. In fact, cooked chicken and pork work too.

Serves 4

10 minutes

5 to 10 minutes

1 tablespoon vegetable oil, or olive oil

2 cloves garlic, minced

1 teaspoon minced fresh ginger

⅓ cup soy sauce

¼ cup light brown sugar

2 tablespoons water

3 ½ to 4 cups cubed cooked steak from the French Onion Steaks (page 127), or any cooked steak

Salt and freshly ground black pepper

Chopped green onions for serving

Toasted sesame seeds for serving,* optional

Sriracha sauce for serving

1. Heat the vegetable oil (or olive oil) in a large skillet or wok over medium heat. Add the garlic and ginger, and cook for 30 seconds, until the garlic and ginger are fragrant. Add the soy sauce, brown sugar, and water, and bring to a simmer. Simmer for 3 minutes, until the liquid reduces slightly.

2. Add the steak to the pan, and simmer for 1 to 2 minutes, until hot and bubbling. Season to taste with salt and black pepper.

3. Top the steak with green onions and sesame seeds (if using), and serve with sriracha sauce on the side.

---

* You can find toasted sesame seeds in the spice aisle, right next to the raw sesame seeds. If you already have raw seeds and want to toast them yourself, place about 2 tablespoons of the seeds in a dry skillet, and set the pan over medium heat. Cook for 2 to 3 minutes, until golden brown, shaking the pan frequently to promote even cooking and to prevent scorching.

SERVING SUGGESTION: I served the steak and sticky sauce over brown rice so I could soak up every drop. You can serve the mixture over any rice variety, Asian noodles, or your favorite grain. For a low-carb meal, serve the beef in lettuce cups.

ONG FOODS, INC.
anyon Rd., Irwindale, CA 91706
46-8328   www.huyfong.com
7 oz. (1 lb. 1 oz.)(481 g)

GOOD TO KNOW

If you don't have leftover steak, you can make this dish with leftover cooked chicken or pork from any recipe in this book or any previous meal.

Korean Short Ribs

Short ribs on a busy weeknight? Yes indeed! Use your blender to quickly make the marinade (a playful combination of juicy pears, salty soy sauce, tangy garlic, sweet mirin, and pungent ginger). Then, use ribs that are cut flanken style (cut across the ribs instead of between them) because they have a shorter cooking time. Added bonus? Flanken-style ribs deliver more meat-to-bone ratio in every bite.

Serves 4, with leftover rib meat for a future meal

10 to 15 minutes

5 to 10 minutes

6 pounds flanken-style short ribs, or English-style short ribs (butterfly English-style short ribs to create long, thin strips of meat)

1 small Asian pear, or regular pear, peeled, cored, and chopped

½ cup chopped onion, any color

½ cup soy sauce

⅓ cup light brown sugar

⅓ cup mirin (Japanese rice wine)

¼ cup water

4 cloves garlic, minced

2 teaspoons sesame oil

1 teaspoon black pepper

1 teaspoon minced fresh ginger

½ teaspoon gochujang, or cayenne pepper

2 teaspoons toasted sesame seeds* for serving

Chopped green onions for serving

1. Rinse the short ribs in cold water to remove any bone fragments, pat them dry, and transfer them to a large shallow dish. Set aside.

2. In a blender or food processor, combine all remaining ingredients except the sesame seeds and green onions, and process until blended. Pour the mixture over the ribs, and turn to coat, working the marinade into the meat with your hands.

3. If you have the time, marinate for 20 minutes or up to 12 hours in the refrigerator.

4. Remove the ribs from the marinade, and discard the marinade.

5. Coat a grill pan, griddle, or outdoor grill with cooking spray (or vegetable oil), and preheat to medium-high.

6. Add the ribs to the hot pan/grill, and cook for 2 to 3 minutes per side, until browned and a meat thermometer registers 200 to 205°F.

7. Reserve about 1 cup of the rib meat for the Short Rib Tostadas with Chipotle-Lime Slaw (page 132) or another future meal. Refrigerate for up to 3 days.

8. Sprinkle the sesame seeds over the remaining ribs, top with green onions, and serve.

---

* You can find toasted sesame seeds in the spice aisle, right next to the raw sesame seeds. If you already have raw seeds and want to toast them yourself, place the seeds in a dry skillet and set the pan over medium heat. Cook for 2 to 3 minutes, until golden brown, shaking the pan frequently to promote even cooking and to prevent scorching.

Round Two

Short Rib Tostadas *with* Chipotle-Lime Slaw

Juicy short rib meat and crunchy radishes piled onto crispy, salty corn tortillas and topped with a creamy, chipotle-spiked coleslaw. There's an unbelievable amount of flavor and texture in this dish, and it comes together in just minutes.

Serves 4

10 to 15 minutes

5 to 7 minutes

FOR THE TOSTADAS:

8 to 12 street taco-size
     corn tortillas

Salt

4 cups sliced short rib meat (bone
     free) from the Korean
     Short Ribs (page 131), or
     any cooked beef, warmed
     in a large skillet over
     medium heat until just hot

½ cup thinly sliced radishes

FOR THE CHIPOTLE-LIME SLAW:

⅓ cup mayonnaise

2 tablespoons minced chipotle
     chiles in adobo sauce

2 tablespoons fresh lime juice

2 tablespoons granulated sugar

3 cups shredded coleslaw
     mix, or a combination of
     shredded green cabbage,
     red cabbage, and carrots

Salt and freshly ground
     black pepper

1. Preheat the oven to 400°F. Line a large baking sheet with parchment paper or aluminum foil.

2. Arrange the tortillas on the prepared pan, spray with cooking spray, and season with salt. Bake for 5 to 7 minutes, until crisp. Set aside.

3. Meanwhile, in a large bowl, whisk together the mayonnaise, chipotle chiles, lime juice, and sugar. Fold in the slaw mix. Season to taste with salt and black pepper.

4. Arrange the tortillas on a flat surface, and top with the short rib meat, slaw, and radishes.

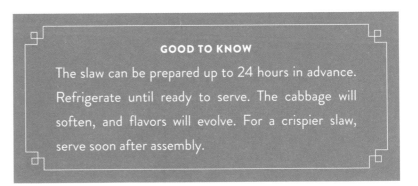

GOOD TO KNOW

The slaw can be prepared up to 24 hours in advance. Refrigerate until ready to serve. The cabbage will soften, and flavors will evolve. For a crispier slaw, serve soon after assembly.

PREP AHEAD TIP: To save time, you can purchase premade tostada shells, which are sold in the Mexican food aisle of the grocery store.

ALSO GOOD TO KNOW

You can make this dish with leftover cooked chicken, steak, or pork from any recipe in this book or any previous meal. You can also use rotisserie chicken meat.

Round One

Pork Chops *with* Apple Salsa

Pork chops and apples have a natural affinity, and this dish showcases the pairing in the most delightful way. First, the chops are marinated in a sweet and tangy blend of apple cider, dijon mustard, and thyme. This lively combination adds great flavor and tenderizes the chops before they're quickly pan-seared. Then, the chops are topped with a colorful blend of sweet and tart apples, red onion, cilantro, and jalapeño—all tossed with honey and lime.

Serves 4, with leftover pork chops for a future meal

15 minutes

10 minutes

FOR THE PORK CHOPS:

2 cups apple cider

1 tablespoon dijon mustard

1 teaspoon dried thyme

Salt and freshly ground black pepper

8 boneless or bone-in pork chops (regular or thick cut), about 5 ounces each, trimmed of fat

1 tablespoon vegetable oil

FOR THE APPLE SALSA:

2 tablespoons fresh lime juice

2 teaspoons honey

1 sweet apple (such as Fuji or Gala), cored and diced

1 tart apple (such as Granny Smith), cored and diced

¼ cup diced red onion

¼ cup chopped fresh cilantro

1 jalapeño, seeded and minced

1. In a large sealable container or baking dish, whisk together the apple cider, dijon mustard, thyme, ½ teaspoon salt, and ¼ teaspoon black pepper. Add the pork chops, and turn to coat. If you have the time, marinate for 15 to 20 minutes or up to 24 hours in the refrigerator.

2. Meanwhile, to make the salsa, in a large bowl, whisk together the lime juice and honey. Add the remaining ingredients, and toss to combine. Season to taste with salt and black pepper. Set aside.

3. Remove the pork chops from the marinade, and discard the marinade.

4. Heat the vegetable oil in a large skillet over medium-high heat. Working in batches to prevent crowding the pan, add the pork chops, and cook for 3 to 4 minutes per side, until browned and a meat thermometer registers 145°F (timing depends on the thickness of your chops).

5. Reserve half of the pork chops for the Spicy Pork Noodle Bowls (page 136) or another future meal. Refrigerate for up to 3 days.

6. Serve the remaining pork chops with the apple salsa spooned over top.

Spicy Pork Noodle Bowls

Nuggets of moist pork and tender rice noodles tossed with salty soy sauce, brown sugar, and a garlic-infused chili sauce. The ingredient list is short, but the flavor profile is huge, and each bite asserts sweetness, saltiness, and a hint of heat.

Serves 4

5 to 10 minutes

5 to 10 minutes

8 ounces rice noodles, also called pad thai noodles

¼ cup soy sauce

2 tablespoons Asian chili garlic sauce, or to taste

2 tablespoons light brown sugar

1 tablespoon fresh lime juice

1 tablespoon rice vinegar, regular or seasoned

2 ½ to 3 cups cubed cooked pork from the Pork Chops with Apple Salsa (page 135), or any cooked pork

Chopped green onions for serving

Lime wedges for serving

1. Cook the rice noodles according to the package directions. Drain, and cover with aluminum foil to keep warm.

2. Meanwhile, in a large skillet, whisk together the soy sauce, chili garlic sauce, sugar, lime juice, and rice vinegar.

3. Set the pan over medium heat, and bring to a simmer. Fold in the noodles and pork, and cook for 2 to 3 minutes to heat through.

4. Top with green onions, and serve with lime wedges on the side.

GOOD TO KNOW

You can make this dish with leftover cooked chicken, steak, shrimp, or scallops from any recipe in this book or any previous meal.

Pork Tenderloin *with* Creamy Mushroom Gravy

Moist pork tenderloin pan-seared until golden and then braised in a creamy, sherry-infused mushroom gravy. The ingredient list is straightforward, the process is easy, and the dish is totally crowd-pleasing!

🍴 Serves 4, with leftover pork tenderloin for a future meal

🥄 10 minutes

🔥 15 to 20 minutes

3 pork tenderloins (about 12 ounces each), cut crosswise into 1-inch thick medallions

Salt and freshly ground pepper

1 tablespoon olive oil

2 tablespoons unsalted butter, divided

4 ounces sliced button or cremini mushrooms

2 cloves garlic, minced

1 teaspoon dried thyme

⅓ cup sherry, marsala, or chicken broth

1 teaspoon dijon mustard

½ cup heavy cream

Chopped fresh parsley for serving

1. Season the pork pieces with salt and black pepper. Heat the olive oil and 1 tablespoon of the butter together in a large skillet over medium-high heat. Add the pork, and cook until lightly browned on both sides. Transfer the pork to a plate.

2. Add the remaining butter to the pan. When the butter is bubbling, add the mushrooms, and cook for 3 to 5 minutes, until soft. Add the garlic and thyme, and stir to coat. Cook for 1 minute, until the garlic and thyme are fragrant. Add the wine (or broth) and dijon mustard, and bring to a simmer. Reduce the heat to low, and add the heavy cream.

3. Return the pork to the pan with any accumulated juices from the plate. Simmer for 3 to 5 minutes, until the pork is cooked through and the sauce thickens.

4. Reserve half of the pork slices (without the mushrooms) for the Sweet-and-Sour Pork (page 140) or another future meal. Refrigerate for up to 3 days.

5. Spoon the mushrooms over the remaining pork slices. Top with fresh parsley, and serve.

SERVING SUGGESTION: This mushroom gravy is so divine, I suggest serving the dish over rice, buttered noodles, or mashed potatoes. A chunk of warm bread on the side would be nice too. To round out the meal, add your favorite raw or steamed vegetable. For more inspiration, check out my Meal Prep 101 tips 23, 24, and 25.

Round Two
Sweet-and-Sour Pork

Juicy chunks of pork tenderloin, glazed with sweet and tangy, garlic-infused plum sauce. The glaze is sticky and finger-lickin' good! Serve the pork and sauce over rice or noodles or in lettuce wraps for one incredible meal.

Serves 4

10 to 15 minutes

5 minutes

1 tablespoon peanut oil, or vegetable oil

2 ½ to 3 cups cubed cooked pork from the Pork Tenderloin with Creamy Mushroom Gravy (page 139), or any cooked pork

2 to 3 cloves garlic, minced

½ cup plum sauce

1 tablespoon mirin (Japanese rice wine)

¼ cup water

1 tablespoon cornstarch

Salt and freshly ground black pepper

Chopped fresh cilantro for serving

1. Heat the peanut oil (or vegetable oil) in a large skillet over medium-high heat. Add the pork, and cook for 2 minutes. Add the garlic, and cook for 30 seconds. Add the plum sauce and mirin, and bring to a simmer.

2. Dissolve the cornstarch in the water, and add the mixture to the pan. Simmer for 2 to 3 minutes, until the sauce thickens. Season to taste with salt and black pepper.

3. Top with fresh cilantro, and serve.

PREP AHEAD TIP: This dish is best served soon after preparing, but you can cut the pork (or chicken/steak) into bite-size pieces and refrigerate for up to 24 hours before cooking.

SERVING SUGGESTION: For a complete and filling meal, serve the pork over rice, noodles, or in lettuce wraps. To round out the meal, add your favorite raw or steamed vegetable. For more inspiration, check out my Meal Prep 101 tips 23, 24, and 25.

SEAFOOD

Round One

Garlic Butter Salmon

Sublimely tender salmon infused with butter, garlic, and fresh lemon and flawlessly roasted in under 15 minutes. The fish is perfectly cooked (fork tender not flaky), and each succulent forkful is equal parts sweet (from the butter), tangy (from the lemon), and nutty (from the garlic).

Serves 4, with leftover salmon for a future meal

10 minutes

10 to 15 minutes

3 pounds salmon fillets, whole or individual fillets

Salt and freshly ground black pepper

4 tablespoons unsalted butter, softened

1 ½ tablespoons fresh lemon juice

2 cloves garlic, minced

Chopped fresh parsley or chives for serving

1. Preheat the oven to 400°F. Coat a shallow baking dish with cooking spray or brush with olive oil.
2. Pat the salmon fillets dry, and transfer them to the prepared pan. Season the salmon with salt and black pepper.
3. In a small bowl, combine the butter, lemon juice, and garlic. Mix until blended. Spread the mixture all over the salmon fillets.
4. Roast for 10 to 15 minutes, until the salmon is fork tender (a meat thermometer should register 145°F).
5. Reserve half of the salmon for the Teriyaki Salmon Ramen Noodles (page 146) or another future meal. Refrigerate for up to 3 days.
6. Top the remaining salmon with fresh parsley or chives, and serve.

SERVING SUGGESTION: For a complete and filling meal, serve the salmon with your favorite raw or steamed vegetable and a starchy side, such as rice, beans, pasta, potatoes, sweet potatoes, quinoa, couscous, or whole grain bread. For more inspiration, check out my Meal Prep 101 tips 23, 24, and 25.

Round Two
Teriyaki Salmon Ramen Noodles

You will never look at a package of ramen noodles the same way after making this sensational meal! The noodles are jazzed up with store-bought teriyaki sauce and then decorated with green peas, crunchy water chestnuts, perfectly cooked eggs, and moist chunks of salmon. Pretty to look at, crazy delicious, and ready in minutes.

Serves 4

10 to 15 minutes

10 minutes

3 packages instant ramen noodles, flavor packets discarded

½ cup frozen peas, kept frozen until ready to use

½ cup sliced water chestnuts

½ cup teriyaki sauce, or my homemade teriyaki sauce below

4 large eggs

2 to 3 cups cooked salmon pieces (2-inch chunks) from the Garlic Butter Salmon (page 145), or any cooked salmon

Chopped green onions for serving

1. Cook the ramen noodles according to the package directions, adding the frozen peas and water chestnuts for the last minute of cooking. Drain, and transfer to a large bowl. Add about ¼ cup of the teriyaki sauce, and toss to coat.

2. Meanwhile, to prepare the eggs, bring about 2 inches of water to a boil in a medium saucepan over high heat. Add the eggs, cover, and cook for 7 minutes. Drain and transfer the eggs to an ice water bath to stop further cooking. When cool enough to handle, peel and halve the eggs.

3. Transfer the noodle mixture to individual shallow bowls, and top with the salmon and halved eggs. Drizzle the remaining teriyaki sauce over top. Top with green onions, and serve.

GOOD TO KNOW
If you feel inspired and have the time, try making my homemade teriyaki sauce (recipe below).

HOMEMADE TERIYAKI SAUCE:

1 cup water, divided

⅓ cup soy sauce

3 tablespoons light
    brown sugar

1 tablespoon rice vinegar,
    regular or seasoned

½ teaspoon ground ginger

¼ teaspoon garlic powder

1 ½ tablespoons cornstarch

Salt and freshly ground
    black pepper

1. In a small saucepan, combine ¾ cup of the water, soy sauce, brown sugar, rice vinegar, ginger, and garlic. Set the pan over medium-high heat, and bring to a simmer. Simmer for 3 to 5 minutes. Dissolve the cornstarch in the remaining ¼ cup of water, and add the mixture to the pan. Simmer for 2 minutes, until the sauce thickens. Season to taste with salt and black pepper.

GOOD TO KNOW

Cajun seasoning is a robust spice blend that typically consists of salt, garlic, onion, paprika, black pepper, cayenne pepper, oregano, thyme, and red pepper flakes. Look for Cajun seasoning in the spice aisle of the grocery store. If you can't find Cajun seasoning, you may also use Creole seasoning.

Cajun Butter Salmon

With just a handful of ingredients, you can create a showstopping, mouth-watering meal in under 20 minutes. In this dish, creamy butter is kicked up with bold Cajun flavors (cayenne, black pepper, oregano, thyme, garlic) and then slightly sweetened with honey. This balance of sweetness and heat is the perfect partner for salmon, and the mixture infuses and caramelizes the fish as it quickly bakes in the oven.

Serves 4, with leftover salmon for a future meal

10 minutes

10 to 15 minutes

3 pounds salmon fillets, whole or individual fillets

Salt and freshly ground black pepper

5 tablespoons unsalted butter, softened

1 tablespoon Cajun seasoning

1 tablespoon honey

Chopped fresh chives or parsley for serving

Lemon wedges for serving

1. Preheat the oven to 400°F. Line a large baking sheet with parchment paper or aluminum foil.

2. Pat the salmon fillets dry and transfer them to the prepared pan. Season the salmon with salt and black pepper.

3. In a small bowl, combine the butter, Cajun seasoning, and honey. Mix until blended. Spread the mixture all over the salmon fillets.

4. Bake for 10 to 15 minutes, until the salmon is fork tender (a meat thermometer should register 145°F).

5. Reserve half of the salmon for the Salmon Taco Bowls (page 152) or another future meal. Refrigerate for up to 3 days.

6. Top the remaining salmon with fresh chives or parsley, and serve with lemon wedges on the side.

Round Two
Salmon Taco Bowls

In this assembly-style meal, fluffy, taco-seasoned rice is topped with moist salmon, fresh tomatoes, green onions, and cilantro. This hearty dish is wholly satisfying and brimming with nutrients. The best part is the flavors of the Cajun seasoning work incredibly well with the ingredients used in taco seasoning (chili powder, cumin, garlic, onion, oregano).

Serves 4

10 minutes

15 minutes

1 cup long grain white rice

2 tablespoons taco seasoning (the powdered mix), divided, plus more for serving

1 tablespoon unsalted butter

2 cups chicken broth, or water

Salt and freshly ground black pepper

2 to 3 cups cooked salmon pieces (2-inch chunks) from the Cajun Butter Salmon (page 151), or any cooked salmon

1 cup cherry tomatoes, grape tomatoes, or regular tomatoes, chopped, for serving

Fresh lettuce leaves or spring mix greens for serving

Lime wedges for serving

Chopped fresh cilantro for serving

Chopped green onions for serving

Hot sauce for serving

1. In a medium saucepan, combine the rice, 1 tablespoon of the taco seasoning, and butter. Add the broth (or water), set the pan over high heat, and bring to a boil. Reduce the heat to low, cover, and cook for 15 to 20 minutes, until the liquid is absorbed and the rice is tender. Fluff with a fork. Season to taste with salt and black pepper.

2. Transfer the rice to individual bowls, and arrange the salmon over top. Sprinkle the salmon with a little taco seasoning. Arrange the tomatoes, lettuce, and lime wedges alongside the salmon. Top with fresh cilantro and green onions, and serve with hot sauce on the side.

SERVING SUGGESTION: This dish is robust enough to be considered a complete meal, but if you want to add heft, serve the taco bowls with flour or corn tortillas on the side.

GOOD TO KNOW

If you don't have leftover salmon, you can make this dish
with leftover cooked seafood, chicken, or steak from any
recipe in this book or any previous meal.

GOOD TO KNOW

As I mentioned, this thick sauce is tremendously versatile, so bookmark this recipe and use the sauce on chicken, steak, pork, fish, and shellfish.

Round One

Sweet-and-Sour Baked Salmon

This baked salmon is glazed with the easiest, most delicious sweet-and-sour sauce ever. The sauce comes together in minutes, in one pan, and features a unique commingling of pineapple juice, soy sauce, brown sugar, ketchup, garlic, and ginger. It's sweet, salty, and completely alive with flavor. In fact, the sauce is so magnificent, you'll want to glaze everything with it.

Serves 4, with leftover salmon for a future meal

10 minutes

10 to 12 minutes

8 salmon fillets, about 5 to 6 ounces each

Salt and freshly ground black pepper

½ cup 100% pineapple juice

2 tablespoons ketchup

2 tablespoons light brown sugar

2 tablespoons rice vinegar, regular or seasoned

2 tablespoons soy sauce

2 teaspoons cornstarch

½ teaspoon garlic powder

⅛ teaspoon ground ginger

Chopped green onions for serving

1. Preheat the oven to 375°F. Coat a shallow baking dish with a thin layer of olive or vegetable oil.

2. Pat the salmon fillets dry and place them in the prepared pan. Season the salmon with salt and black pepper. Set aside.

3. In a small saucepan, whisk together the pineapple juice, ketchup, brown sugar, rice vinegar, soy sauce, cornstarch, garlic, and ginger. Set the pan over medium heat, and bring to a simmer. Cook for 2 to 3 minutes, until the sauce thickens, stirring frequently.

4. Spoon the sauce over the salmon.

5. Bake for 10 to 15 minutes, until the salmon is fork tender (a meat thermometer should register 145°F).

6. Reserve half of the salmon for the Salmon Niçoise Salad (page 156) or another future meal. Refrigerate for up to 3 days.

7. Top the remaining salmon with the green onions, and serve.

ALSO GOOD TO KNOW
You can make this dish spicy by adding hot sauce or sriracha sauce to the glaze. You can also top the finished dish with crushed red pepper flakes.

Round Two
Salmon Niçoise Salad

Tuna might be the classic addition to this French salad, but salmon works equally well and enlivens the plate with its distinct flavor and color. This salad features moist chunks of salmon, tender-crisp green beans, baby potatoes, crisp cucumbers, and briny olives and capers. Then, everything is tossed with a refreshing, homemade dressing of lemon juice, dijon mustard, and olive oil.

Serves 4

15 minutes

10 to 15 minutes

FOR THE DRESSING:

⅓ cup olive oil

3 tablespoons fresh lemon juice

1 tablespoon dijon mustard

Salt and freshly ground
    black pepper

FOR THE SALAD:

1 pound baby potatoes,
    rinsed and patted dry

½ pound green beans, ends
    trimmed and halved

4 large eggs

2 to 3 cups cooked salmon
    pieces (2-inch chunks)
    from the Sweet-and-Sour
    Baked Salmon (page 155),
    or any cooked salmon

1 cup sliced English/
    seedless cucumber,
    peeled or unpeeled

½ cup kalamata (Greek)
    olives, pitted and halved

2 tablespoons drained capers

Fresh parsley leaves for serving

1. To make the dressing, whisk together the olive oil, lemon juice, and dijon mustard. Season to taste with salt and black pepper. Set aside.

2. To prepare the potatoes and green beans, place the whole potatoes in a large saucepan, and pour over enough water to cover by about 2 inches. Set the pan over high heat, and bring to a boil. Reduce the heat to medium-high, and cook for 10 minutes, until the potatoes are fork tender, adding the green beans for the last 2 minutes of cooking. Drain, and toss the potatoes and green beans with about half of the dressing.

3. To prepare the eggs, bring about 2 inches of water to a boil in a medium saucepan over high heat. Add the eggs, cover, and cook for 7 minutes. Drain, and transfer the eggs to an ice water bath to stop further cooking. When cool enough to handle, peel and halve the eggs.

4. Arrange the potatoes and green beans in salad bowls, and top with the salmon, eggs, cucumber, olives, and capers. Drizzle the remaining dressing over top, and garnish with fresh parsley.

GOOD TO KNOW

If you don't have leftover salmon, you can use canned salmon, smoked salmon, or leftover cooked fish or shellfish from any recipe in this book or any previous meal.

Round One

Tuna *with* Roasted Red Pepper Salsa

Perfectly cooked tuna—golden on the outside, pink on the inside—topped with a smoky blend of roasted red peppers, fresh cilantro, green onions, cumin, and lime. This meal is incredibly yummy, undeniably healthy, and super easy to make.

Serves 4, with leftover tuna for a future meal

10 minutes

5 to 10 minutes

1 cup chopped roasted red peppers, from water-packed jar

¼ cup chopped fresh cilantro

¼ cup chopped green onions

2 tablespoons fresh lime juice

1 teaspoon ground cumin

Salt and freshly ground black pepper

6 tuna steaks, about 5 to 6 ounces each

1. To make the salsa, in a medium bowl, combine the roasted red peppers, cilantro, green onions, lime juice, and cumin. Mix well. Season to taste with salt and black pepper. Set aside.

2. Coat a stove-top grill pan, griddle, or large skillet with olive oil, and preheat to medium-high.

3. Season both sides of the tuna with salt and black pepper, and add to the hot pan. Cook for 2 to 3 minutes per side for medium-rare or longer for more fully cooked tuna.

4. Reserve 2 tuna steaks for the Tuna Couscous Salad (page 160) or another future meal. Refrigerate for up to 3 days.

5. Serve the remaining tuna with the salsa spooned over top.

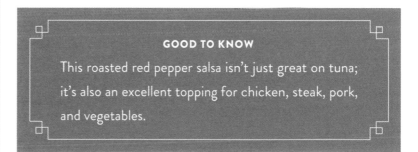

GOOD TO KNOW
This roasted red pepper salsa isn't just great on tuna; it's also an excellent topping for chicken, steak, pork, and vegetables.

Round Two

Tuna Couscous Salad

Fluffy balls of semolina pasta tossed in a lemon vinaigrette and topped with chunks of tuna, briny kalamata olives, vibrant parsley, and salty feta cheese. There's an undeniable amount of flavor and texture in this whimsical meal. And it couldn't be easier to make.

Serves 4

10 to 15 minutes

10 minutes

2 cups pearled couscous

¼ cup olive oil

3 tablespoons fresh
     lemon juice

1 teaspoon dijon mustard

1 clove garlic, minced or grated

1 teaspoon dried oregano

Salt and freshly ground
     black pepper

2 cups cooked tuna pieces
     (2-inch chunks) from
     the Tuna with Roasted
     Red Pepper Salsa
     (page 159), or any
     cooked tuna or salmon

½ cup kalamata (Greek) olives,
     pitted and chopped

¼ cup chopped fresh parsley

2 tablespoons crumbled
     feta cheese

1. Cook the couscous according to the package directions.

2. Meanwhile, in a small bowl, whisk together the olive oil, lemon juice, dijon mustard, garlic, oregano, ½ teaspoon salt, and ¼ teaspoon black pepper.

3. Transfer the couscous to a large bowl, add the dressing, and toss to coat. Fold in the tuna, olives, and parsley. Season to taste with salt and black pepper.

4. Transfer the mixture to a serving bowl, top with the feta, and serve.

GOOD TO KNOW

If you don't have leftover tuna, you can make this dish with leftover cooked seafood, chicken, or steak from any recipe in this book or any previous meal.

GOOD TO KNOW

This recipe works with any firm-fleshed white fish, including flounder, halibut, tilapia, catfish, striped bass, whitefish, haddock, and scrod. It also works with shellfish, including shrimp and scallops.

Round One

Roasted Miso Cod

Sweet, savory, and boasting the perfect amount of umami, this fish dish is mind-blowing. The coating is a simple blend of miso, sugar, mirin, and soy sauce, but the balance of salty and sweet is unrivaled. As the fish bakes, the miso flavor deepens and evolves, and the sugar caramelizes slightly. This is a restaurant-worthy dish, made in the comfort of your own kitchen.

Serves 4, with leftover cod for a future meal

10 minutes

10 to 12 minutes

8 cod fillets, about 5 to
    6 ounces each
½ cup white or red miso paste
3 tablespoons mirin
    (Japanese rice wine)
3 tablespoons granulated sugar
1 tablespoon soy sauce
1 tablespoon vegetable oil
Freshly ground black pepper
Sliced green onions for
    serving, optional

1. Preheat the oven to 450°F. Coat a shallow baking dish or baking sheet with parchment paper or a thin layer of vegetable oil.

2. Pat the cod fillets dry, and place them, skin side down, in the prepared pan. Set aside.

3. In a small bowl, whisk together the miso paste, mirin, sugar, soy sauce, and vegetable oil. Brush the mixture all over the cod. Season the top with black pepper. If you have the time, marinate for 10 to 15 minutes (no need to refrigerate).

4. Roast for 10 to 12 minutes, until the top of the cod is browned and a thin skewer or knife inserts easily through the middle, without any resistance.

5. If necessary, use tweezers to remove any pin bones (there should be no resistance if the fish is fully cooked).

6. Reserve 4 of the cod fillets for the Creamy Fish Chowder with Potatoes and Corn (page 164) or another future meal. Refrigerate for up to 3 days.

7. Top the remaining cod with green onions (if using), and serve.

ALSO GOOD TO KNOW

White and red miso paste are sold in the Asian food aisle of the grocery store and Asian specialty food markets. Either one will work in this dish (I used white miso paste).

Seafood · 163

Round Two

Creamy Fish Chowder
with Potatoes *and* Corn

Chowder might be the ultimate comfort food, and this dish completely illustrates that fact. Tender pieces of white fish are simmered in a rich yet light thyme-infused, creamy broth with onions, garlic, and gold potatoes. Just before serving, chewy-crisp bacon is nestled on top, rounding out the flavor spectrum and making a fantastic presentation.

Serves 4

10 to 15 minutes

15 to 20 minutes

1 tablespoon olive oil

4 green onions, white and green parts separated and chopped

2 cloves garlic, minced

2 tablespoons all-purpose flour

2 cups chicken broth

2 cups half-and-half

2 medium Yukon gold potatoes, peeled and cubed

1 teaspoon dried thyme

Salt and freshly ground black pepper

2 to 3 cups cooked cod pieces (2-inch chunks) from the Roasted Miso Cod (page 163), or any cooked white fish

1 cup fresh or frozen corn kernels, kept frozen until ready to use

3 slices bacon, cooked until chewy-crisp and chopped

1. Heat the olive oil in a large stock pot or saucepan over medium-high heat. Add the white part of the green onions, and cook for 2 to 3 minutes, until soft. Add the garlic, and cook for 30 seconds.

2. Add the flour, and stir to coat.

3. Add the broth, half-and-half, potatoes, thyme, ½ teaspoon salt, and ¼ teaspoon black pepper, and bring to a boil.

4. Reduce the heat to medium-low, and simmer for 5 minutes.

5. Add the cod, corn, and most of the bacon (leave some for garnish), and simmer for 5 minutes, until the potatoes are fork tender. Season to taste with salt and black pepper.

6. Ladle the soup into bowls, and top with the green portion of the green onions and remaining bacon.

PREP AHEAD TIP: Cook your bacon in advance and store the strips in a freezer bag in the freezer for up to 3 months. It's great to have cooked bacon on hand, especially when you just need a few slices at a time. I always cook an entire pound of bacon at once (roasted on a parchment-lined baking sheet for 15 minutes at 400°F). When you're ready to use the bacon, simply reheat it in the microwave for 30 to 60 seconds or in a 300-degree oven for 5 to 10 minutes.

GOOD TO KNOW

If you don't have leftover cod, you can use any white fish—fresh or frozen, cooked or uncooked. When starting with raw seafood, add a few minutes to the cooking time.

Round One
Baked Halibut Packets *with* Rosemary

Packet cooking, which is a classic way to steam fish, is the best way to guarantee sublimely tender fish every time. In this recipe, halibut fillets are seasoned with butter, lemon, and rosemary, and baked to perfection in about 15 minutes. Because the fish is sealed in a packet with the flavor elements, it's infused with deliciousness all the way through. And cleanup couldn't be easier!

Serves 4, with leftover halibut for a future meal

15 minutes

14 to 16 minutes

8 halibut fillets, about 5 to 6 ounces each

Salt and freshly ground black pepper

8 teaspoons unsalted butter

8 slices lemon, about ¼-inch-thick rounds

8 rosemary sprigs (about 4-inches long)

Lemon wedges for serving

1. Preheat the oven to 400°F.
2. Arrange eight 12- to 14-inch pieces of parchment paper on a flat surface. Arrange the halibut fillets on the center of each piece.
3. Season the halibut with salt and black pepper. Top each fish fillet with 1 teaspoon of the butter. Arrange a lemon slice on the butter, and then top with a sprig of rosemary.
4. Lift the parchment paper on opposite sides to meet in the middle, above the fish. Tightly fold and roll the paper until it reaches the fish. Pull up the ends, and crimp to seal. Transfer the packets to a large baking sheet, and bake for 14 to 16 minutes, until the fish is fork tender and opaque throughout.
5. Reserve half of the halibut for the Halibut Lettuce Wraps with Chipotle Cream (page 168) or another future meal. Refrigerate for up to 3 days.
6. Serve the remaining halibut with lemon wedges on the side.

Round Two

Halibut Lettuce Wraps
with Chipotle Cream

This gluten-free, ultra-fresh dish features buttery lettuce, moist halibut, creamy avocado, and sweet red onion, all topped with a smoky, chipotle-spiked sour cream. There's just enough smoky heat in the sour cream to enhance the fish, not overpower it.

🍴 Serves 4

🥄 15 minutes

½ cup sour cream

1 tablespoon minced chipotle chiles in adobo sauce, or more/less to taste

1 teaspoon avocado oil, or olive oil

½ teaspoon ground cumin

Salt and freshly ground black pepper

8 leaves butterhead lettuce (butter or bibb), or romaine lettuce

2 to 3 cups cooked halibut pieces (2-inch chunks) from the Baked Halibut Packets with Rosemary (page 167), or any cooked fish

1 avocado, pitted and diced

½ cup thinly sliced red onion

Paprika for serving

Lime wedges for serving

1. In a small bowl, whisk together the sour cream, chipotle chiles, avocado oil (or olive oil), and cumin. Season to taste with salt and black pepper.

2. Fill the lettuce leaves with the halibut, avocado, and red onion. Sprinkle with a little paprika, and serve with the chipotle cream and lime wedges on the side.

> **GOOD TO KNOW**
>
> If you don't have leftover halibut, you can make this dish with leftover cooked seafood, chicken, or steak from any recipe in this book or any previous meal. You can also use rotisserie chicken meat.

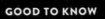

Baked White Fish
with Parmesan Crust

Fork-tender, buttery fish topped with a sweet, crunchy coating of mayonnaise, parmesan cheese, and panko breadcrumbs. There are very few ingredients in this recipe, but flavors and textures are off the hook (sorry for the pun)! The slightly sweet mayo caramelizes and partners perfectly with the salty parmesan cheese, toasted panko, and grassy green onions.

Serves 4, with leftover fish for a future meal

15 minutes

8 to 10 minutes

1 ½ cups panko breadcrumbs

1 cup grated parmesan cheese

¼ cup mayonnaise

4 teaspoons chopped green onions

Salt and freshly ground black pepper

8 firm-fleshed white fish fillets, about 5 to 6 ounces each

Chopped fresh parsley for serving

1. Preheat the oven to 400°F. Line a large baking sheet with parchment paper or aluminum foil.

2. In a medium bowl, combine the breadcrumbs, parmesan cheese, mayonnaise, and green onions. Mix well, and set aside.

3. Pat the fish fillets dry, and transfer them to the prepared pan. Season the top with salt and black pepper.

4. Top the fillets with the panko mixture, and press down gently to create a crust.

5. Bake for 8 to 10 minutes, until a meat thermometer registers 125 to 130°F.

6. Remove the pan from the oven, and preheat the broiler.

7. Place the pan under the broiler (about 4 inches from the heat source), and broil for 1 to 2 minutes, until the crust is golden brown and the fish is fork tender.

8. Reserve 4 of the fish fillets (about 2 cups of fish pieces) for the Fish Salad with Pesto (page 172) or another future meal. Refrigerate for up to 3 days.

9. Top the remaining fish fillets with fresh parsley, and serve.

Fish Salad *with* Pesto

You will love the uniqueness of this refreshing salad. The parmesan crust from the Baked White Fish with Parmesan Crust (page 171) marries perfectly with the parmesan cheese, garlic, basil, and pine nuts in the pesto. And since we use store-bought pesto, this wildly flavorful meal comes together in under 15 minutes.

🍴 Serves 4

🥄 15 minutes

2 tablespoons prepared basil pesto, plus more for serving

2 tablespoons fresh lemon juice

4 cups sliced kale or mixed greens of choice (when using kale, remove the tough stems)

Salt and freshly ground black pepper

2 cups cooked white fish pieces (2-inch chunks) from the Baked White Fish with Parmesan Crust (page 171), or any cooked fish

½ cup cherry or grape tomatoes, halved

1. In a large bowl, whisk together the pesto and lemon juice. Add the kale (or mixed greens), and toss to coat. Season to taste with salt and black pepper. Transfer the greens to a salad bowl, and top with the fish and tomatoes. If desired, drizzle a little more pesto over top before serving.

GOOD TO KNOW
I used kale in this recipe, but any mixed greens, baby spinach, and/or lettuce varieties will work.

ALSO GOOD TO KNOW

If you don't have leftover white fish, you can make this dish with leftover cooked seafood or chicken from any recipe in this book or any previous meal.

GOOD TO KNOW

If you don't have shrimp, you can make this dish
with scallops, chicken, or medallions of pork.

Round One

Honey Hoisin Shrimp

It's not often you can find (and serve) a four-ingredient dish with so much flavor! This succulent shrimp is glazed with a sweet-and-salty combination of store-bought hoisin sauce and honey. The hoisin sauce is salty, and the honey complements and balances that essence in the most wonderful way. The glaze is sticky and rich and coats every inch of the plump shrimp.

Serves 4, with leftover shrimp for a future meal

10 minutes

5 minutes

⅓ cup hoisin sauce

¼ cup honey

¼ cup soy sauce

1 tablespoon vegetable oil

3 pounds tail-on shrimp
    (16 to 20 count),
    peeled and deveined,
    defrosted if frozen

Salt and freshly ground
    black pepper

Chopped fresh cilantro for
    serving, optional

1. In a small bowl, whisk together the hoisin sauce, honey, and soy sauce. Set aside.
2. Heat the vegetable oil in a large skillet over medium-high heat. Add the shrimp, and cook for 2 minutes, turning occasionally. Season the shrimp with salt and black pepper.
3. Add the hoisin sauce mixture, and bring to a simmer. Simmer for 2 minutes, until the shrimp is opaque and cooked through and sauce thickens and coats the shrimp like a glaze.
4. Reserve half of the shrimp for the Shrimp Cakes with Honey Lemon Aioli (page 176) or another future meal. Refrigerate for up to 3 days.
5. Top the remaining shrimp with fresh cilantro (if using), and serve.

SERVING SUGGESTION: Since the sauce in this dish is packed with flavor, I suggest you serve the shrimp with rice or Asian noodles. For a low-carb dish, serve the shrimp in lettuce leaves.

Shrimp Cakes *with* Honey Lemon Aioli

These tender shrimp patties are completely fabulous. The outside is toasty and crisp, and the moist inside boasts a playful combination of tender shrimp, bell pepper, and chives. The sweet cakes are perfectly complemented with a refreshing, slightly tart combination of mayo, lemon, and honey.

Serves 4

15 minutes

8 to 10 minutes

FOR THE SHRIMP CAKES:

1 pound cooked shrimp from the Honey Hoisin Shrimp (page 175), or any cooked shrimp, tails removed

¼ cup panko breadcrumbs

¼ cup diced red bell pepper

1 tablespoon chopped fresh chives, plus more for serving

1 large egg

Salt and freshly ground black pepper

4 tablespoons olive oil

FOR THE HONEY LEMON AIOLI:

½ cup mayonnaise

1 tablespoon fresh lemon juice

1 teaspoon honey

1 teaspoon grated fresh lemon zest

1. Place the shrimp in a food processor, and pulse on and off until coarsely chopped. Add the breadcrumbs, bell pepper, chives, egg, ½ teaspoon salt, and ¼ teaspoon black pepper, and pulse on and off until blended; you should be able to squeeze a small amount of the mixture and it will hold its shape.

2. Form the mixture into 4 patties, each about 1-inch thick.

3. Heat the olive oil in a large skillet over medium-high heat. Add the shrimp patties, and cook for 4 to 5 minutes per side, until golden brown and cooked through.

4. To make the aioli, whisk together all the ingredients until blended. Season to taste with salt and black pepper.

5. Spoon the lemon aioli over the shrimp cakes, and top with fresh chives.

GOOD TO KNOW

The shrimp cakes can be assembled and refrigerated for up to 24 hours before cooking. The aioli can be prepared up to 24 hours in advance. Refrigerate until ready to serve.

GOOD TO KNOW

If you don't have shrimp, you can make this dish with scallops or chicken.

Round One

Brown Butter Shrimp

Plump and sweet shrimp, tossed in a garlic-infused, nutty brown butter that's enhanced with sweet wine and tangy lemon. This is a restaurant-worthy meal, but it's made with a handful of ingredients and ready in under 20 minutes.

Serves 4, with leftover shrimp for a future meal

10 minutes

5 to 7 minutes

4 tablespoons unsalted butter

3 cloves garlic, minced

3 pounds tail-on shrimp
(16 to 20 count),
peeled and deveined,
defrosted if frozen

¼ cup white wine, or vermouth

1 ½ tablespoons fresh
lemon juice

Salt and freshly ground
black pepper

2 tablespoons chopped
fresh parsley

½ teaspoon crushed red
pepper flakes, or
more/less to taste

1. Melt the butter in a large skillet over medium heat. Cook until foamy and light brown. Add the garlic, and cook for 30 seconds. Add the shrimp, and cook for 3 minutes, turning frequently. Add the white wine (or vermouth) and lemon juice, and cook until the liquid evaporates and the shrimp is opaque and cooked through. Season the shrimp with salt and black pepper.

2. Reserve half of the shrimp for the Shrimp Soft Tacos with Spicy Slaw (page 180) or another future meal. Refrigerate for up to 3 days.

3. Top the remaining shrimp with fresh parsley and red pepper flakes, and serve.

SERVING SUGGESTION: For a complete and filling meal, serve the shrimp with your favorite raw or steamed vegetable and a starchy side, such as rice, noodles, potatoes, sweet potatoes, quinoa, couscous, or whole grain bread. For more inspiration, check out my Meal Prep 101 tips 23, 24, and 25.

Shrimp Soft Tacos *with* Spicy Slaw

Every bite of these scintillating tacos transports you straight to Mexico. The shrimp is infused with zesty taco seasoning and served on soft flour tortillas with a creamy, fiery slaw made with coleslaw mix, mayonnaise, cilantro, jalapeño, and lime. The dish is fresh, exciting, healthy, and ready in under 20 minutes.

Serves 4

15 minutes

2 to 3 minutes

FOR THE SPICY SLAW:

⅓ cup mayonnaise

2 tablespoons fresh lime juice

2 tablespoons granulated sugar

2 cups shredded coleslaw mix

½ jalapeño, seeded and minced

2 tablespoons chopped
	fresh cilantro

Salt and freshly ground
	black pepper

FOR THE SHRIMP SOFT TACOS:

1 pound cooked shrimp from
	the Brown Butter Shrimp
	(page 179), or any cooked
	shrimp, tails removed

2 tablespoons taco seasoning
	(the powdered mix)

1 tablespoon olive oil

8 to 12 street taco-size
	flour or corn tortillas,
	warmed if desired

1 avocado, pitted and diced

Lime wedges for serving

1. To make the spicy slaw, in a large bowl, whisk together the mayonnaise, lime juice, and sugar. Fold in the slaw mix, jalapeño, and fresh cilantro. Season to taste with salt and black pepper. Set aside.

2. To prepare the shrimp, in a large bowl, combine the shrimp and taco seasoning. Toss to coat.

3. Heat the olive oil in a large skillet over medium heat. Add the shrimp, and cook for 2 to 3 minutes to heat through.

4. Serve the shrimp in the tortillas with the spicy slaw, avocado, and lime wedges on the side.

GOOD TO KNOW

These soft tacos are also fabulous with leftover cooked seafood, chicken, steak, and pork from any recipe in this book or any previous meal.

ALSO GOOD TO KNOW

If you don't have leftover shrimp, you can use any pre-cooked shrimp. To save money, look for precooked shrimp in the frozen foods section of the grocery store.

Round One
Maple Soy Scallops

Juicy, pan-seared scallops shimmering in a sweet, tangy, and fiery sauce of soy, maple syrup, and sriracha. Ready in minutes, ultra-healthy, and super easy to make. You are going to love this salty-sweet glaze. It's got the perfect balance of flavors (salty soy + sweet maple), and there's a hint of tangy heat from sriracha sauce and dijon mustard. Plus, it's not just excellent with these scallops; it works with salmon, shrimp, and chicken too.

Serves 4, with leftover scallops for a future meal

10 minutes

8 to 10 minutes

¼ cup soy sauce

3 tablespoons pure maple syrup

2 teaspoons dijon mustard

2 teaspoons sriracha sauce, plus more for serving

3 pounds large sea scallops (about 28 to 30), muscles removed

2 tablespoons unsalted butter, divided

Salt and freshly ground black pepper

2 teaspoons toasted sesame seeds*

Chopped green onions for serving, optional

1. In a small bowl, whisk together the soy sauce, maple syrup, dijon mustard, and sriracha sauce. Set aside.

2. Pat the scallops dry using a double layer of paper towels, pressing down gently to remove excess water.

3. Heat 1 tablespoon of butter in a large skillet over medium-high heat. When the butter is bubbling, add half of the scallops, and cook in a single layer until golden brown and just cooked through, about 2 to 3 minutes per side. Season the scallops with salt and black pepper. Repeat with the second half of the scallops and remaining butter.

4. Reserve half of the scallops for the Pasta with Scallops and White Wine Sauce (page 184) or another future meal. Refrigerate for up to 3 days.

5. Add the soy mixture to the same skillet over medium-low heat. Simmer for 2 to 3 minutes, until the mixture thickens to a glaze. Return the remaining half of the scallops to the skillet, and toss to coat. Top with sesame seeds and green onions (if using), and serve.

* You can find toasted sesame seeds in the spice aisle, right next to the raw sesame seeds. If you already have raw seeds and want to toast them yourself, place the seeds in a dry skillet and set the pan over medium heat. Cook for 2 to 3 minutes, until golden brown, shaking the pan frequently to promote even cooking and to prevent scorching.

SERVING SUGGESTION: This syrupy glaze is fantastic, so I suggest serving the scallops and sauce with rice, Asian noodles, or your favorite grain. For a low-carb meal, serve the scallops in lettuce leaves.

Pasta with Scallops and White Wine Sauce

Strands of tender pasta tossed in a garlicky, wine-infused cream sauce, topped with seared scallops and shredded parmesan cheese. The cream sauce is rich, the scallops are sweet, and the cheese is salty and nutty—which translates to a delightful balance of flavors on the palate.

Serves 4

10 to 15 minutes

10 minutes

12 ounces linguine, or pasta of choice

1 tablespoon unsalted butter

1 tablespoon olive oil

3 to 4 cloves garlic, minced

1 cup white wine

1 cup heavy cream, or half-and-half

⅓ cup shredded parmesan cheese, plus more for serving

12 to 16 cooked scallops from the Maple Soy Scallops (page 183), or any cooked scallops or shrimp (about ¾ pound cooked)

Salt and freshly ground black pepper

Chopped fresh parsley for serving

1. Cook the pasta according to the package directions, reserving ½ cup of the pasta water (this is just in case you need it later). Drain, and cover with aluminum foil to keep warm.

2. Meanwhile, heat the butter and olive oil together in a large skillet over medium heat. Add the garlic, and cook for 30 seconds. Add the wine, and bring to a simmer. Simmer for 3 to 5 minutes, until the wine reduces by half.

3. Add the heavy cream (or half-and-half) and parmesan cheese, and return to a simmer. Simmer for 2 to 3 minutes, until the sauce thickens, stirring constantly.

4. Fold in the pasta, adding some of the reserved pasta water if you desire a thinner sauce. Gently fold in the scallops, and cook for 1 to 2 minutes to heat through.

5. Top with fresh parsley, and serve with extra parmesan cheese on the side.

PASTA AND RICE

Pasta Round One

Spaghetti *with* Pink Vodka Sauce

This satisfying dish boasts tender noodles in a satiny blend of tomato sauce, cream, and vodka. And the vodka serves a culinary purpose; the alcohol acts as a solvent and brings out specific flavors in tomatoes that are not released in water or fat. It's this simple addition that brings the dish to an entirely new level. That said, if you'd rather skip the vodka, you can certainly leave it out.

Serves 4, with leftover spaghetti for a future meal

10 minutes

15 minutes

2 pounds spaghetti, or pasta of choice

2 cups tomato sauce

¼ cup vodka, optional

1 tablespoon olive oil

1 teaspoon dried basil

¼ teaspoon garlic powder

½ teaspoon onion powder

Salt and freshly ground black pepper

½ cup heavy cream, or half-and-half

Chopped fresh basil or parsley for serving

Grated parmesan cheese for serving

1. Cook the spaghetti according to the package directions. Drain, and reserve half for the Vegetable Pad Thai (page 190) or another future meal. Refrigerate for up to 3 days. Cover the remaining spaghetti with aluminum foil to keep warm.

2. Meanwhile, in a large saucepan or high-sided skillet, combine the tomato sauce, vodka, olive oil, dried basil, garlic powder, onion powder, ½ teaspoon salt, and ¼ teaspoon black pepper. Set the pan over medium heat, and bring to a simmer. Simmer for 10 minutes, stirring frequently. Reduce the heat to low, and stir in the heavy cream (or half-and-half). Cook for 1 to 2 minutes. Fold in the spaghetti, and cook for 1 minute to heat through. Season to taste with salt and black pepper.

3. Transfer the spaghetti to serving bowls, and top with the fresh basil or parsley and parmesan cheese.

ALSO GOOD TO KNOW

I used spaghetti here because I love how the long noodles luxuriate in the sauce from end to end. Feel free to use any pasta shape you have on hand.

Pasta Round Two
Vegetable Pad Thai

Silky noodles tossed in a sweet and tangy sauce and then invigorated with garlic, ginger, bell peppers, eggs, and crunchy peanuts. A squeeze of lime and the entire flavor spectrum hits your palate. I love the balance of flavors here—salty, tangy, and sweet. If you want to add spicy, you can serve the dish with hot sauce on the side.

Serves 4

10 to 15 minutes

10 minutes

¼ cup soy sauce

¼ cup tamarind puree, or mango chutney

1 tablespoon rice vinegar, regular or seasoned

1 tablespoon tomato paste

2 teaspoons peanut oil

1 teaspoon sesame oil

½ cup thinly sliced white onion

1 bell pepper, any color, seeded and thinly sliced

2 cloves garlic, minced

1 teaspoon minced fresh ginger

1 pound cooked spaghetti from the Spaghetti with Pink Vodka Sauce (page 189), or any cooked pasta

2 large eggs, lightly beaten

¼ cup fresh cilantro leaves

¼ cup dry-roasted salted peanuts, coarsely chopped

Lime wedges for serving

1. In a small bowl, whisk together the soy sauce, tamarind puree (or mango chutney), rice vinegar, and tomato paste. Set aside.

2. Heat the peanut and sesame oils together in a large skillet over medium heat. Add the onion, bell pepper, garlic, and ginger, and cook for 3 to 5 minutes, until soft.

3. Add the spaghetti, and toss to combine. Add the soy sauce mixture, reduce the heat to medium, and cook for 3 to 5 minutes, until the pasta is heated through.

4. Push the spaghetti to one side of the pan to make room for the eggs. Add the eggs, and cook until scrambled and still moist. Fold the eggs into the spaghetti.

5. Top the spaghetti and vegetables with the fresh cilantro and peanuts, and serve with lime wedges on the side.

GOOD TO KNOW

Pad thai is typically made with rice noodles, but it's equally amazing with spaghetti. For a gluten-free dish, choose rice noodles or gluten-free spaghetti.

Pasta Round One

Linguine *with* Lemon *and* Asparagus

Asparagus and lemon have a natural affinity, and when you partner the two with buttery, garlicky pasta and salty cheese, you create a dish that sings to you. The trick to heightened flavor in this dish is the caramelized lemons. Getting a golden brown sear on the lemons sweetens them slightly while preserving their tang, and it's those two nuances that simultaneously add depth and levity to this meal.

🍴 Serves 4, with leftover linguine for a future meal

🥄 10 to 15 minutes

🔥 10 to 15 minutes

2 pounds linguine, or
    pasta of choice

1 bunch asparagus spears,
    woody ends trimmed and
    cut into 2-inch pieces

2 lemons, sliced into
    ½ inch thick rounds

2 tablespoons olive oil, plus
    more for coating the pan

3 tablespoons unsalted
    butter, divided

2 cloves garlic, minced

1 teaspoon dried oregano

¼ cup grated parmesan cheese,
    plus more for serving

2 tablespoons chopped
    fresh parsley or basil

Salt and freshly ground
    black pepper

1. Cook the linguine according to the package directions, adding the asparagus for the last 2 minutes of cooking. Drain, reserving 1 cup of the pasta water.

2. Reserve 4 cups of the linguine for the Linguine Frittata (page 196) or another future meal. Refrigerate for up to 3 days. Cover the remaining linguine and asparagus with aluminum foil to keep warm.

3. Coat a large skillet with a thin layer of olive oil (just enough to grease the pan). Set the pan over medium-high heat. Add the lemons to the hot pan, and sear until golden brown on both sides. Transfer the lemons to a plate, and set aside.

4. Heat the olive oil and 2 tablespoons of the butter together in the same skillet over medium heat. When the butter is bubbling, add

GOOD TO KNOW
This dish is a perfectly satisfying vegetarian meal, but feel free to add cooked chicken or shellfish for added protein.

the garlic and oregano, and cook for 30 seconds. Stir in the linguine and asparagus, reserved pasta water, and parmesan cheese. Toss to combine.

5. Fold in the remaining tablespoon of butter and fresh parsley or basil.

6. Season to taste with salt and black pepper.

7. Top the linguine with the seared lemons, and serve with extra parmesan cheese on the side.

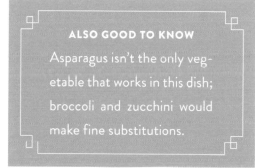

Pasta Round Two

Linguine Frittata

Pasta in a frittata? Yes, you read that correctly, and you may never look at a frittata the same way again. This baked egg dish is astonishing from top to bottom. The core of the frittata is a blend of seasoned eggs, linguine, and store-bought marinara sauce. Once the mixture is partially cooked on the stove top, it's topped with mozzarella and parmesan cheeses and finished in the oven. The result? A golden-brown bottom, moist middle, and cheesy top. I think you'll find that all ages will adore this one.

Serves 4

15 minutes

5 to 10 minutes

6 large eggs

¼ cup half-and-half

1 teaspoon dried basil or oregano

½ teaspoon garlic powder

Salt and freshly ground black pepper

1 tablespoon olive oil

1 pound cooked linguine from the Linguine with Lemon and Asparagus (page 193), or any cooked pasta

1 cup marinara sauce of choice, or my homemade marinara sauce from the Parmesan Chicken Fingers with Marinara (page 59)

½ cup shredded mozzarella cheese

2 tablespoons grated parmesan cheese, plus more for serving

Chopped fresh basil for serving, optional

1. Preheat the oven to 375°F.

2. In a large bowl, whisk together the eggs, half-and-half, basil (or oregano), garlic powder, ½ teaspoon salt, and ¼ teaspoon black pepper. Set aside.

3. Heat the olive oil in a large (10- to 12-inch) oven-safe skillet over medium heat. Add the linguine, and reheat quickly, tossing to coat the noodles with oil while keeping them from browning. Add the marinara sauce, and toss to coat.

4. Add the egg mixture, and shake the pan to settle the eggs around the pasta. Cook for 3 to 5 minutes, until the egg starts to set around the edges of the pan and is almost set in the middle (there should be about ¼- to ½-inch of uncooked egg on the surface). Sprinkle the mozzarella and parmesan cheeses over top.

5. Transfer the pan to the oven, and bake for 5 to 10 minutes, until the egg is set and the cheese melts. Top with fresh basil (if using), and serve.

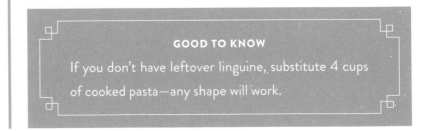

GOOD TO KNOW

If you don't have leftover linguine, substitute 4 cups of cooked pasta—any shape will work.

Pasta Round One

Garlic Parmesan Pasta
with Toasted Black Pepper

With its tender strands of pasta laced with garlic, parmesan cheese, and toasted black pepper, this dish is similar to cacio e pepe, the classic Italian dish that features pasta, parmesan cheese, and black pepper. In this version, I toss the noodles with an easy, buttery sauce of pasta water, parmesan cheese, and copious amounts of freshly ground, toasted black pepper. A handful of fresh parsley just before serving puts the dish over the top.

Serves 4, with leftover pasta for a future meal

5 to 10 minutes

15 minutes

2 pounds pasta of choice (I used fettuccine for this dish and penne for Round Two)

2 teaspoons freshly ground black pepper

5 tablespoons unsalted butter, divided

3 tablespoons olive oil

1 clove garlic, minced

1 cup grated parmesan cheese, plus more for serving

2 tablespoons chopped fresh parsley

Salt

1. Cook the pasta according to the package directions. Drain, reserving 1 ¼ cups of the pasta water. Reserve half of the pasta for the Pasta with Sausage and Broccoli (page 200) or another future meal. Refrigerate for up to 3 days. Cover the remaining pasta with aluminum foil to keep warm.

2. Toast the ground pepper in a large, dry skillet over medium heat until fragrant—this should take about 30 to 60 seconds. Add 4 tablespoons of the butter, olive oil, and garlic, and cook until the butter melts, about 1 minute.

3. Add the drained pasta, 1 cup of the reserved pasta water, and the parmesan cheese. Toss to coat the pasta well. Add the remaining ¼ cup of reserved pasta water and tablespoon of butter, and toss to coat.

4. Fold in the fresh parsley. Season with salt, and serve with extra parmesan cheese on the side.

ALSO GOOD TO KNOW

Thirty seconds in a dry skillet turns regular ground black pepper into its toasted form, which enriches its aroma and brings out more of a spicy, smoky essence.

Pasta Round Two

Pasta *with* Sausage *and* Broccoli

Tender pasta, colorful broccoli, and savory sausage—that's all you need to create this mouthwatering, comforting meal. The ingredient list is short, but flavors soar thanks to the complexity of the sausage. And the best part is this dish is customizable. You can choose mild or hot sausage, and the sausage can be made with pork, chicken, or turkey. Vegan sausage works too!

Serves 4

10 minutes

10 to 15 minutes

1 pound sweet or spicy Italian sausage, casing removed

2 to 3 cloves garlic, minced

3 to 4 cups fresh or frozen broccoli florets, kept frozen until ready to use

1 ½ cups chicken broth

Salt and freshly ground black pepper

3 tablespoons unsalted butter

1 pound cooked pasta from the Garlic Parmesan Pasta with Toasted Black Pepper (page 199), or any cooked pasta (I used penne)

½ cup grated parmesan cheese

1. Brown the sausage in a large, high-sided skillet over medium-high heat, breaking up the meat as it cooks. Add the garlic, and cook for 30 seconds.

2. Add the broccoli, broth, ½ teaspoon salt, and ¼ teaspoon black pepper, and bring to a simmer. Simmer for 3 to 4 minutes, until the broccoli is tender-crisp, scraping up any browned bits from the bottom of the pan and incorporating them into the sauce. Add the butter, and simmer for 2 minutes, until the sauce thickens slightly.

3. Fold in the pasta and parmesan cheese. Cook for 1 to 2 minutes to heat through. Season to taste with salt and black pepper, and serve.

PREP AHEAD TIP: To save prep time, purchase ground sausage instead of the links.

GOOD TO KNOW

Feel free to use your favorite vegetables here. I chose broccoli, but you can also use green beans, green peas, asparagus, spinach, kale, tomatoes, and more.

Cheesy Baked Rigatoni
with Chipotle Sausage

There's layer upon layer of flavor in this dish—tender tubes of pasta, sausage-spiked tomato sauce, and melty mozzarella cheese. It's the smoky chipotle sausage that truly catapults this dish. In fact, you need very few additional herbs and spices because there's so much flavor in the meat.

Serves 4, with leftover pasta for a future meal

10 minutes

20 minutes

2 pounds rigatoni, or pasta of choice

1 pound chipotle sausage, or sausage of choice, casing removed

2 cloves garlic, minced

1 teaspoon dried basil

1 teaspoon dried oregano

Salt and freshly ground black pepper

3 ½ cups tomato sauce

2 cups shredded mozzarella cheese, divided

2 tablespoons chopped fresh parsley or basil

1. Preheat the oven to 350°F. Coat a 9-by-13-inch baking dish with cooking spray.

2. Cook the rigatoni according to the package directions. Drain, reserving ½ cup of the pasta water. Reserve half of the pasta for the Rigatoni with Blistered Tomatoes and Spinach (page 206) or another future meal. Refrigerate for up to 3 days. Cover the remaining rigatoni with aluminum foil to keep warm.

3. Meanwhile, brown the sausage in a large saucepan or high-sided skillet over medium-high heat, breaking up the meat as it cooks. Add the garlic, basil, oregano, ½ teaspoon salt, and ¼ teaspoon black pepper, and cook for 30 seconds, until the herbs are fragrant.

4. Add the tomato sauce, and bring to a simmer. Fold in the cooked rigatoni and reserved ½ cup pasta water. Remove the pan from the heat.

5. Spoon half of the mixture into the prepared pan. Top with half of the mozzarella cheese.

6. Spoon the remaining rigatoni mixture over top, and top with the remaining mozzarella cheese.

7. Cover with a lid or aluminum foil (spray the aluminum foil with

cooking spray to prevent sticking), and bake for 15 minutes. Uncover, and bake for 5 more minutes, until the mixture is bubbling and the cheese melts.

8. Top with fresh parsley or basil, and serve.

GOOD TO KNOW

While I adore smoky chipotle sausage in this recipe, you can use any sausage variety you prefer, including Italian, sweet, hot, turkey, chicken, and vegan.

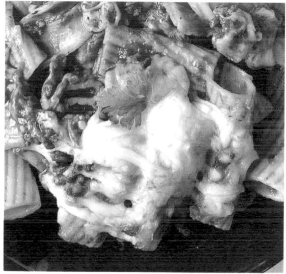

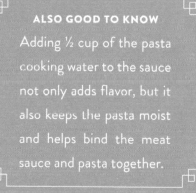

Pasta Round Two

Rigatoni *with* Blistered Tomatoes *and* Spinach

If you've never blistered tomatoes before, now's the time. Roasting tomatoes until they caramelize and blister brings out their sweetness and softens their acidity. It is such a simple process but yields a huge transformation. In this dish, the sweet, softened tomatoes are partnered with cooked pasta, baby spinach, parmesan cheese, and a tangy balsamic vinaigrette. It's a colorful and playful party on the palate.

Serves 4

10 to 15 minutes

10 to 15 minutes

3 cups cherry or grape
    tomatoes
3 tablespoons olive oil, divided
Salt and freshly ground
    black pepper
4 cups baby spinach leaves,
    packed, stems removed
2 tablespoons balsamic vinegar
1 teaspoon dijon mustard
1 pound cooked rigatoni
    from the Cheesy Baked
    Rigatoni with Chipotle
    Sausage (page 203),
    or any cooked pasta
⅓ cup grated parmesan cheese

1. Preheat the oven to 400°F. Line a large baking sheet with parchment paper or aluminum foil.

2. Place the tomatoes in a large bowl, add 1 tablespoon of the olive oil, and toss to coat. Transfer the tomatoes to the prepared pan, and season with salt and black pepper.

3. Roast for 10 to 15 minutes, until the tomatoes are blistered.

4. Meanwhile, place the spinach in a large bowl. Remove the blistered tomatoes from the oven, and immediately place them on top of the spinach, without stirring. Allow the tomatoes to steam the spinach for 1 to 2 minutes, until wilted.

5. In a small bowl, whisk together the remaining 2 tablespoons of olive oil, balsamic vinegar, and dijon mustard.

6. Add the pasta and balsamic vinaigrette to the tomatoes and spinach, and toss gently to combine. Fold in the parmesan cheese. Season to taste with salt and black pepper, and serve.

GOOD TO KNOW

Any pasta shape works in this dish, so feel free to use a variety you already have on hand.

ALSO GOOD TO KNOW

In this recipe, we take advantage of the hot tomatoes and use them to steam/soften the fresh spinach leaves, so make sure you transfer the tomatoes from the oven directly to the spinach.

ONE MORE THING

This vegetarian dish can be served warm, room temperature, or chilled, which makes it a great option for picnics, tailgates, and other outdoor parties.

Pasta Round One

Bow Tie Carbonara

This quick-and-easy weeknight meal features bow tie (farfalle) pasta in a garlicky cream sauce that's studded with salty bacon bits and showered with parmesan cheese. What makes the sauce extra special? Egg yolks. Used to thicken the sauce, the egg yolks also add unrivaled richness.

Serves 4, with leftover pasta for a future meal

10 to 15 minutes

10 to 15 minutes

2 pounds bow tie pasta, or pasta of choice

3 tablespoons olive oil

4 to 5 strips bacon of choice (including turkey bacon and meatless/plant-based bacon), diced, or 4 ounces pancetta, diced

¼ cup diced shallot, or white onion

2 cloves garlic, minced

1 ½ cups heavy cream

4 large egg yolks

2 tablespoons grated parmesan cheese, plus more for serving

Salt and freshly ground pepper

2 tablespoons chopped fresh parsley

1. Cook the pasta according to the package directions. Drain, reserving ¼ cup of the pasta water. Reserve half of the pasta for the Pasta Salad with Sun-Dried Tomato-Basil Pesto (page 210) or another future meal. Refrigerate for up to 3 days. Cover the remaining pasta with aluminum foil to keep warm.

2. Meanwhile, heat the olive oil in a large skillet over medium-high heat. Add the bacon (or pancetta), and cook until chewy-crisp. Add the shallot (or white onion) and garlic, and cook for 1 minute. Reduce the heat to medium, and add the heavy cream. Simmer for 2 minutes, until the sauce thickens slightly.

3. Add the pasta and reserved cooking water, and cook for 1 minute to heat through. Reduce the heat to low, and stir in the egg yolks and parmesan cheese. Cook for 1 minute, until the sauce is thick and creamy.

4. Season to taste with salt and black pepper.

5. Top with fresh parsley, and serve with extra parmesan cheese on the side.

Pasta Round Two

Pasta Salad *with* Sun-Dried Tomato-Basil Pesto

Pasta salad is one of those dishes that can be served differently every time—and everyone will love the latest iteration. In this recipe, we turn leftover cooked pasta into something vibrant, fresh, and colorful by adding pesto, sun-dried tomatoes, bell peppers, and mozzarella. It's sweet, tangy, salty, and creamy and delivers a color, texture, and flavor burst in every bite.

Serves 4

15 minutes

⅓ cup prepared basil pesto

¼ cup drained oil-packed
    sun-dried tomatoes

1 tablespoon olive oil, or
    oil from the sun-
    dried tomato jar

1 pound cooked bow tie
    pasta from the Bow Tie
    Carbonara (page 209),
    or any cooked pasta

1 bell pepper, any color,
    seeded and chopped

½ cup cherry or grape
    tomatoes, halved

4 to 6 ounces fresh mozzarella,
    cut into bite-size pieces
    (you can also use ciliegine,
    or small balls of fresh
    mozzarella, quartered)

2 tablespoons chopped
    fresh basil

Salt and freshly ground
    black pepper

1. In a blender or food processor, combine the pesto, sun-dried toma-toes, and olive oil (or sun-dried tomato oil). Process until blended, leaving little bits of sun-dried tomato if desired. Transfer the mix-ture to a large bowl, add the pasta, and toss to coat.

2. Fold in the bell pepper, tomatoes, mozzarella, and fresh basil. Season to taste with salt and black pepper, and serve.

GOOD TO KNOW

This vegetarian dish can be served warm, room tempera-ture, or chilled, which makes it a great option for school lunch, work lunch, and outdoor parties and picnics.

GOOD TO KNOW

If you want to ramp up protein, add 2 cups of diced or shredded cooked chicken (after you reserve 2 cups of the rice mixture for the Minestrone Soup).

Rice Round One

Cheesy Mexican Rice *and* Beans

Raid your spice rack for this one! Fluffy rice is scented with onion, garlic, chili powder, oregano, and cilantro, tossed with savory beans, and then topped with sharp and stretchy cheese. Main dish and/or side dish, this is one the whole family (and all your friends) will adore.

Serves 4, with leftover rice for a future meal

10 minutes

15 to 20 minutes

1 tablespoon olive oil

½ cup chopped onion, any color

2 to 3 cloves garlic, minced

2 cups long grain white rice

1 tablespoon chili powder

1 teaspoon dried cilantro

1 teaspoon dried oregano

Salt and ground black pepper

4 cups chicken broth, or vegetable broth, or water

1 (15-ounce) can seasoned black beans, or chili beans of choice, undrained

¾ cup shredded Mexican cheese blend, or blend of cheddar and monterey jack cheeses

Chopped green onions for serving

1. Heat the olive oil in a large saucepan over medium-high heat. Add the onion, and cook for 3 to 5 minutes, until soft. Add the garlic, and cook for 30 seconds.

2. Add the rice, chili powder, cilantro, oregano, ½ teaspoon salt, and ¼ teaspoon black pepper, and stir to coat. Cook for 1 minute to toast the rice and release the essence from the herbs and spices, stirring constantly. Add the broth (or water), and bring to a simmer. Reduce the heat to low, cover, and cook for 15 to 20 minutes, until the liquid is absorbed and the rice is tender. Fold in the beans.

3. Remove the pan from the heat, and reserve 2 cups of the rice mixture for the Hearty Minestrone (page 214) or another future meal. Refrigerate for up to 3 days.

4. Top the remaining rice mixture with the cheese, cover with foil or a lid, and let stand for a few minutes to melt the cheese.

5. Top with green onions, and serve.

ALSO GOOD TO KNOW

I used long grain white rice in this recipe, but you can use your favorite rice variety, including brown, jasmine, basmati, or Texmati.

Rice Round Two

Hearty Minestrone

The actual definition of comfort, this bowl of bliss is bursting with fresh vegetables, fluffy rice, tangy tomatoes, and a sublime herbal broth. And since we're using the rice from the Cheesy Mexican Rice and Beans (page 213), all the flavor is already built in, which means very little prep work for you.

Serves 4

10 to 15 minutes

15 minutes

1 tablespoon olive oil

1 cup chopped carrots

1 cup chopped celery

1 medium zucchini, quartered
    lengthwise and cut
    into bite-size pieces

1 teaspoon Italian seasoning

3 cups chicken broth, or
    vegetable broth

1 (28-ounce) can crushed
    tomatoes

2 to 2 ½ cups cooked rice
    and beans from the
    Cheesy Mexican Rice
    and Beans (page 213), or
    any cooked rice or pasta

Salt and freshly ground
    black pepper

Chopped fresh parsley
    for serving

1. Heat the olive oil in a large saucepan over medium-high heat. Add the carrots, celery, and zucchini, and cook for 3 to 5 minutes, until soft. Add the Italian seasoning, and stir to coat. Cook for 1 minute, until the herbs are fragrant.

2. Add the broth and crushed tomatoes, and bring to a simmer. Simmer for 5 minutes. Add the rice and beans, and simmer for 5 minutes to heat through. Season to taste with salt and black pepper.

3. Ladle the soup into bowls, and top with fresh parsley.

GOOD TO KNOW

Feel free to use any vegetables you have in your fridge and/or freezer, and if you don't have leftover rice from the Cheesy Mexican Rice and Beans, you can use 2 cups of cooked rice or pasta.

SERVING SUGGESTION: In my family, we like to top our minestrone soup with grated or shredded parmesan cheese, so serve some on the side if desired.

Rice Round One
Cilantro Lime Rice

This refreshing side dish is alive with flavor thanks to the commingling of fresh green onions, garlic, cilantro, and lime. Be warned, this side dish is so invigorating, it may steal the show.

Serves 4, with leftover rice for a future meal

5 to 10 minutes

15 to 20 minutes

4 cups chicken broth, vegetable broth, or water

2 cups long grain white rice, or jasmine rice

1 tablespoon unsalted butter

3 green onions, white and green parts separated and chopped

2 cloves garlic, minced

¼ cup chopped fresh cilantro

1 ½ tablespoons fresh lime juice

1 tablespoon olive oil

1 teaspoon grated fresh lime zest

Salt and freshly ground black pepper

1. In a medium saucepan, combine the broth (or water), rice, butter, white parts of the green onion, and garlic. Set the pan over high heat, and bring to a boil. Reduce the heat to low, cover, and cook for 15 to 20 minutes, until the liquid is absorbed and the rice is tender.

2. Add the cilantro and lime juice to the rice. Reserve half of the rice for the Lemony Chicken and Rice Soup (page 218) or another future meal. Refrigerate for up to 3 days.

3. Add the olive oil, green part of the green onions, and lime zest to the remaining rice. Toss to combine. Season to taste with salt and black pepper.

SERVING SUGGESTION: You can easily turn this rice dish into a main dish by adding cooked chicken, steak, seafood, or shellfish.

Rice Round Two
Lemony Chicken *and* Rice Soup

Lemon and lime meld together in this delightfully satisfying soup. The lime comes from the Cilantro Lime Rice (page 217), and it adds an additional layer of tanginess to this lemony soup. The simple addition of two aromatic herbs—oregano and bay leaves—transforms the broth into a savory soup while complementing the essence of cilantro. No leftover rice? No problem. Use 2 cups of cooked rice (any variety) instead.

Serves 4

5 to 10 minutes

20 minutes

1 tablespoon olive oil

1 cup chopped carrots

1 cup chopped celery

½ cup chopped onion, any color

2 cloves garlic, minced

6 cups chicken broth, or vegetable broth

2 bay leaves

1 teaspoon dried oregano

2 cups cubed cooked chicken

2 cups cooked rice from the Cilantro Lime Rice (page 217), or any cooked rice

¼ cup fresh lemon juice

¼ cup grated parmesan cheese, plus more for serving

Salt and freshly ground black pepper

Chopped fresh parsley for serving

1. Heat the olive oil in a large saucepan over medium-high heat. Add the carrots, celery, and onion, and cook for 3 to 5 minutes, until soft. Add the garlic, and cook for 30 seconds.

2. Add the broth, bay leaves, and oregano, and bring to a simmer. Simmer for 10 minutes. Remove the bay leaves, and stir in the chicken and rice. Cook for 5 minutes to heat through.

3. Fold in the lemon juice and parmesan cheese. Season to taste with salt and black pepper.

4. Ladle the soup into bowls, and top with fresh parsley. Serve with extra parmesan cheese on the side.

GOOD TO KNOW
You can make this dish with leftover cooked chicken from any recipe in this book or any previous meal. You can also use rotisserie chicken meat.

ALSO GOOD TO KNOW

For a vegetarian soup, simply leave out the chicken. Thanks to the addition of onion, carrots, celery, garlic, and lots of parmesan cheese, this soup has enough heft to stand on its own without the chicken.

GOOD TO KNOW

It's important to rinse the rice before making this dish. Why? Jasmine rice is starchy, and rinsing it removes excess starch and prevents clumping and gumminess. This is especially important here because we're cooking the rice in thick coconut milk.

Rice Round One
Coconut Rice

This creamy rice dish is equal parts sweet and savory, and it makes an excellent side dish (or base) for Asian and Indian dishes. The ingredient list might seem impossibly short for a delectable dish, but the coconut milk adds both sweetness and nuttiness and infuses every grain of rice with its essence.

Serves 4, with leftover rice for a future meal

5 minutes

15 to 20 minutes

2 cups jasmine rice, or long grain white rice

1 (13.5-ounce) can coconut milk, not coconut cream

1 ½ cups water

Salt and freshly ground black pepper

Chopped fresh cilantro for serving

1. Place the rice in a fine mesh sieve, and rinse under cold water until the water runs clear. Drain well.
2. In a medium saucepan, combine the rice, coconut milk, water, and 1 teaspoon of salt. Set the pan over medium-high heat, and bring to a boil. Reduce the heat to low, cover, and cook for 15 to 20 minutes, until the liquid is absorbed and the rice is tender.
3. Fluff with a fork. Season to taste with salt and black pepper.
4. Reserve half of the rice for the Perfect Fried Rice (page 222) or another future meal. Refrigerate for up to 3 days.
5. Top the remaining rice with fresh cilantro, and serve.

SERVING SUGGESTION: You can easily turn this coconut rice into a complete meal by topping it with cooked chicken, steak, seafood, or pork.

Rice Round Two
Perfect Fried Rice

This better-than-takeout fried rice is sure to become a regular part of your menu rotation. It's quick and easy and delivers a fun array of flavors and textures. Whether you start with precooked/leftover rice or make a batch just for this recipe, this winning dish is sure to please the troops at the table. The rice is fluffy, the vegetables are sweet and aromatic, the sauce is savory, and the sesame oil and sesame seeds add nuttiness and crunch.

Serves 4

10 to 15 minutes

10 to 15 minutes

2 tablespoons unsalted
    butter, divided
2 large eggs, lightly beaten
½ cup chopped carrots
½ cup chopped onion, any color
1 bell pepper, any color,
    seeded and chopped
3 cloves garlic, minced
2 cups cooked rice from
    the Coconut Rice
    (page 221), preferably
    chilled, or any cooked rice
5 tablespoons soy sauce,
    plus more if needed
1 teaspoon sesame oil
½ cup frozen peas, kept frozen
    until ready to use
Salt and freshly ground
    black pepper
Chopped green onions
    for serving
Toasted sesame seeds
    for serving*

1. Heat 1 tablespoon of the butter in a large wok or skillet over medium-high heat. Add the eggs, and cook until scrambled and still moist. Transfer the eggs to a plate.

2. Heat the remaining butter in the same pan over medium-high heat. Add the carrots, onion, and bell pepper, and cook for 3 to 5 minutes, until soft. Add the garlic, and cook for 30 seconds.

3. Add the rice, and toss to combine. Add the soy sauce and sesame oil, and cook for 2 minutes, stirring to coat the rice with the sauce. Add the peas, and cook for 1 to 2 minutes, until hot. Fold in the cooked eggs.

4. Season to taste with salt and black pepper (and more soy sauce if desired). Top with green onions and sesame seeds, and serve.

---

*   You can find toasted sesame seeds in the spice aisle, right next to the raw sesame seeds. If you already have raw seeds and want to toast them yourself, place about 2 tablespoons of the seeds in a dry skillet, and set the pan over medium heat. Cook for 2 to 3 minutes, until golden brown, shaking the pan frequently to promote even cooking and to prevent scorching.

PREP AHEAD TIP: Fried rice comes together quickly, so have all your ingredients chopped and ready to go before you start cooking.

222 · 30-Minute Meal Prep

Rice Round One

Spanish Rice

This tasty, colorful side dish transforms rice into something truly remarkable. Scented with chili powder and cumin, the fluffy grains are embellished with onion, bell pepper, garlic, and tomato sauce. The dish is rich yet light and makes an excellent side dish for tacos, enchiladas, fajitas, and grilled and roasted meat, poultry, and seafood.

Serves 4, with leftover rice for a future meal

10 minutes

20 minutes

2 tablespoons vegetable oil

½ cup chopped onion, any color

½ red bell pepper, seeded and chopped

2 cloves garlic, minced

2 cups long grain white rice

2 ½ cups chicken broth, or vegetable broth

1 cup tomato sauce

1 teaspoon chili powder

½ teaspoon ground cumin

Salt and freshly ground black pepper

Chopped green onions for serving

1. Heat the vegetable oil in a large skillet over medium-high heat. Add the onion and bell pepper, and cook for 3 to 5 minutes, until soft. Add the garlic, and cook for 30 seconds.

2. Add the rice, and cook for 2 to 3 minutes, until golden brown, stirring frequently. Add the broth, tomato sauce, chili powder, cumin, ½ teaspoon salt, and ¼ teaspoon black pepper, and bring to a simmer.

3. Reduce the heat to low, cover, and cook for 15 minutes, until the liquid is absorbed and the rice is tender. Fluff with a fork.

4. Reserve half of the rice for the Spinach and Artichoke Rice Bake (page 226) or another future meal. Refrigerate for up to 3 days.

5. Top the remaining rice with green onions, and serve.

SERVING SUGGESTION: This enjoyable side dish can quickly become a main dish by adding cooked chicken, steak, pork, or seafood.

Rice Round Two

Spinach *and* Artichoke Rice Bake

Like hot spinach dip catapulted, this complete vegetarian meal is crammed with flavor thanks to the Spanish Rice (page 225). We take the built-in flavor of onion, garlic, and bell pepper, plus the warming nuances of chili powder and cumin, and enhance the dish with cream cheese, spinach, artichoke hearts, and mozzarella and parmesan cheeses. This is an unbelievable dish that's not only great for a busy weeknight but would also make a great dish for entertaining.

Serves 4

10 to 15 minutes

15 to 20 minutes

2 cups cooked rice from the Spanish Rice (page 225), or any cooked rice

1 (14-ounce) can artichoke hearts, drained and chopped

1 (10- to 12-ounce) package frozen chopped spinach, thawed and well drained to remove all water from the spinach

1 (8-ounce) package cream cheese, softened

1 ½ cups shredded mozzarella cheese, divided

½ cup shredded or grated parmesan cheese, divided

Chopped fresh parsley for serving

1. Preheat the oven to 325°F. Coat a shallow 7-by-11-inch baking dish with cooking spray.
2. In a large bowl, combine the rice, artichokes, spinach, cream cheese, 1 cup of the mozzarella cheese, and ¼ cup of the parmesan cheese. Mix well.
3. Transfer the mixture to the prepared pan, and top with the remaining mozzarella and parmesan cheeses. Bake uncovered for 15 to 20 minutes, until the mixture is hot and the top is golden brown.
4. Top with fresh parsley, and serve.

GOOD TO KNOW

This dish can be considered a complete meal, but if you want added protein, fold in 2 cups of cooked chicken or shrimp when you combine all the ingredients.

Rice Round One
Greek Rice Bowls

This light and satisfying meal is brimming with flavor from the bottom of the bowl to the top. Lemony rice, moist chicken, fresh tomatoes and onion, and salty olives and feta, all drizzled with a creamy, garlicky, dill-infused yogurt dressing. Healthy, easy, gluten-free, and ready in minutes.

Serves 4, with leftover rice for a future meal

15 minutes

15 minutes

2 cups long grain white rice

1 tablespoon olive oil, or unsalted butter

1 teaspoon dried oregano

Salt and freshly ground black pepper

1 teaspoon grated fresh lemon zest

FOR THE DRESSING:

2 cups plain Greek yogurt

1 cup chopped English/seedless cucumber, peeled or unpeeled

2 tablespoons chopped fresh dill

2 tablespoons fresh lemon juice

2 cloves garlic, minced or grated

1 tablespoon olive oil

FOR THE BOWLS:

2 cups cubed cooked chicken

1 cup kalamata (Greek) olives, pitted and sliced

1 cup cherry or grape tomatoes, halved

½ cup sliced red onion

½ cup crumbled feta cheese

Lemon wedges for serving

1. To make the rice, in a medium saucepan, combine the rice, olive oil (or butter), oregano, ½ teaspoon salt, and ¼ teaspoon black pepper. Add 2 cups of water, and set the pan over high heat. Bring to a boil, reduce the heat to low, cover, and cook for 15 minutes, until the liquid is absorbed and the rice is tender. Fold in the lemon zest and fluff with a fork.

2. Reserve 2 cups of the rice for the Mushroom Risotto (page 230) or another future meal. Refrigerate for up to 3 days.

3. Meanwhile, to make the dressing, combine all ingredients in a medium bowl, and mix well. Season to taste with salt and black pepper.

4. Transfer the remaining rice to shallow bowls, and top with the chicken, tomatoes, olives, and red onion. Sprinkle the feta cheese over top. Garnish with lemon wedges, and serve with the dressing on the side.

> **ALSO GOOD TO KNOW**
> If you use the tzatziki from the Mediterranean Meatballs with Tzatziki (page 93), you can skip making the dressing.

SERVING SUGGESTION: If desired, serve the rice bowls with pita pockets or pita chips on the side.

Mushroom Risotto

Yes, you can make risotto with long grain rice! It's not customary, but it works in this recipe because we're repurposing leftover/extra rice from the Greek Rice Bowls (page 229). Since the rice is precooked, you can achieve the same creaminess you get from short grain/arborio rice in a fraction of the time. I think you'll be amazed at the result here—a satiny risotto that features earthy mushrooms and onions in a wine-infused, parmesan-spiked cream sauce.

Serves 4

10 minutes

15 to 20 minutes

4 tablespoons unsalted butter, divided

1 tablespoon olive oil

8 ounces sliced button or cremini mushrooms

¼ cup chopped shallots, or white onion

2 cloves garlic, minced

Salt and freshly ground black pepper

¼ cup white wine

2 cups cooked rice from the Greek Rice Bowls (page 229), or any cooked rice

1 cup vegetable broth, or chicken broth

½ cup heavy cream

½ cup grated parmesan cheese, plus more for serving

Olive oil for drizzling over top

Fresh parsley leaves for serving

1. Heat 3 tablespoons of the butter and the olive oil in a large saucepan over medium-high heat. Add the mushrooms and shallots (or white onion), and cook for 3 to 5 minutes, until soft. Add the garlic, ½ teaspoon salt, and ¼ teaspoon black pepper, and stir to coat. Cook for 1 minute, until the garlic is fragrant.

2. Add the wine, and simmer for 2 minutes, until the liquid is mostly evaporated, scraping up any browned bits from the bottom of the pan and incorporating them into the sauce.

3. Add the rice and broth, and bring to a simmer. Cook until the liquid is absorbed, stirring frequently. Add the heavy cream and parmesan cheese, and cook for 3 to 5 minutes, until the mixture is smooth and creamy, stirring frequently. Fold in the remaining tablespoon of butter. Transfer to a serving bowl, and drizzle a little olive oil over top.

4. Top with fresh parsley, and serve with extra parmesan cheese on the side.

Closing Thoughts

This cookbook has a very special place in my heart. I crafted, tested, and photographed every recipe, and after each meal was complete, I served dinner. Flipping through these pages is a peek inside my real-life kitchen because this book genuinely reflects my day-to-day routine. It's as if I've invited you to dinner...and I can't wait to nosh with you.

Going through the process of writing this book made one thing abundantly clear—mealtime can be easy, whether you've got an arsenal of ingredients on deck (and a well-thought-out plan for using them) or not. That's why I'm so excited to share this work with you. I'm hopeful (and confident) that every meal you build, from this day forward, will be purposeful, affordable, nourishing, and completely sensational.

And let's not forget, the kitchen is the quintessential gathering place, a place to break bread and catch up on life. I'm thrilled you've joined me here so we can embark on this culinary journey together. Pull up a chair, open your pantry and fridge, and let's get cooking.

Index

Note: Page numbers in italic refer to illustrations.

About the Author

Robin Miller has been a TV personality, food writer, nutritionist, and spokesperson since 1990, and she is the author of ten other books, including the *New York Times* bestseller *Quick Fix Meals*.

Robin hosted six seasons of *Quick Fix Meals* on Food Network, and the entire video library is currently streaming on Discovery+ and Amazon Prime Video. Robin also hosts dozens of shows for the popular streaming platform Craftsy, and her content ranges from efficient weeknight cooking to baking like a pro.

Robin writes regular food cover stories for *USA Today*, the *Arizona Republic*, and Mashed. She also posts food content daily and has thousands of recipes on her *Robin Miller Cooks* blog and website.

Robin has a master's degree in food and nutrition from New York University, and she ranks in the top three of famous nutritionists worldwide.

Robin is the proud mom of two young men, and she currently resides in Newtown, Pennsylvania.